¡Mira!

Anneli McLachlan

3

Verde

THE CITY OF PORTSMOUTH GIRLS' SCHOOL
ST. MARY'S ROAD
PORTSMOUTH
PO1 5PF

www.heinemann.co.uk
✓ Free online support
✓ Useful weblinks
✓ 24 hour online ordering

01865 888080

Heinemann

C000133449

Heinemann is an imprint of Pearson Education Limited, a company incorporated in England and Wales, having its registered office at Edinburgh Gate, Harlow, Essex, CM20 2JE. Registered company number: 872828

www.heinemann.co.uk

Heinemann is a registered trademark of Pearson Education Limited

© Pearson Education Limited 2008

First published 2008

13 12 11 10 09 08
10 9 8 7 6 5 4 3 2 1

British Library Cataloguing in Publication Data is available from the British Library on request.

ISBN 978 0 435391 64 5

Copyright notice

All rights reserved. No part of this publication may be reproduced in any form or by any means (including photocopying or storing it in any medium by electronic means and whether or not transiently or incidentally to some other use of this publication) without the written permission of the copyright owner, except in accordance with the provisions of the Copyright, Designs and Patents Act 1988 or under the terms of a licence issued by the Copyright Licensing Agency, Saffron House, 6–10 Kirby Street, London EC1N 8TS (www.cla.co.uk). Applications for the copyright owner's written permission should be addressed to the publisher.

Edited by Kathryn Tate
Managing Editor: Lia Peinador
Designed by Ken Vail Graphic Design, Cambridge
Typeset by Ken Vail Graphic Design, Cambridge
Original illustrations © Pearson Education Limited 2008
Illustrated by Graham Cameron Illustration (David Benham), Ken Laidlaw, Sylvie Poggio Artists Agency (Adz, Mark Ruffle, Rory Walker), Young Digital Poland.
Cover photo © Robert Harding World Imagery/Marco Simoni
Printed in Great Britain by Scotprint

Acknowledgements

Heinemann and the author would like to thank Liliana Acosta Uribe, Clive Bell, Gillian Eades, Alex Harvey, Naomi Laredo, Christopher Lillington, Ana Machado, Lía Peinador and Iñaki Alegre. They would also like to thank Ojos de Brujo, Eroski (www.consumer.es), Fairtrade (www.fairtrade.org.uk), Alfredo Martín Hillera, Smart Set (jazz music, p12), Colegio Santa María La Real (Pamplona), Andrés Larambere, Maika Cáceres, José Manuel Ubani, Laura Osaba, Elena Alegre, Eva Alegre, Unai Sueskun, Xabi Elizalde, Ana Tirapu, Jose Mari Elizalde, Raquel Elizalde, Íñigo Chivite, Míkel Zamacona, Leyre Bardina, Eva Leoz, Amaya Guelbenzu, Juan Oscáriz of Restaurante Josecho, Daniel Fernández, Pedro Jiménez, Beatriz Manrique of Boutique Ellas, María and Laura of boutique Minx, Alomai of La Dolce Vita, José María Bazán and David Garzón of Nordqvist Productions and all those involved with the recordings for their invaluable help in the development and trialling of this course.

The author and publisher would like to thank the following individuals and organisations for permission to reproduce photographs:

Kobal Collection p**11** (James Bond poster); Corbis/Reuters/Pool/Adam Butler p**13** (Murray Perahia); Photoshot/Starstock/David Wimsett (Amy Winehouse);Photoshot/Starstock/Scanpix (Kanye West); Alamy/Karl Hedner (Franz Ferdinand); Corbis/Tim Mosenfelder (Hot Chip); Ojos de Brujo p21 (Ojos de Brujo); Alamy/Jupiter Images/Creatas p**24**(school uniform); Getty Images /PhotoDisc p**27** (Rico); Pearson Education Ltd/Gareth Boden p**27** (Antonio, Carol); iStockphoto.com /David Mathios p**79** (mountains); Dreamstime /Marco Regalia p**79** (volcano); Rex Features/Peter Oxford/ Nature Picture Library p**79** (river Amazon); iStockphoto.com/Jose Carlos Pires Pereira p**79** (desert); iStockphoto.com p**79** (Amazonian jungle); iStockphoto.com/Jose Carlos Pires Pereira p**79** (plains); Alamy/Sean Sprague p**82** (Magali); Alamy/Paul Kingsley p**83** (Carlos); Alamy/Brand X Pictures p**84** (Diego); Corbis/Stephanie Maze p**84** (Mexico City); PA/Empics Sport/Peter Robinson p**86** (Diego Maradona); Photoshot/Landov/Dennis van Tine p**87** (Shakira); Rex Features/Jim Smeal p**87** (Gael Garcia Bernal); Getty Images/PhotoDisc p**89** (Jorge); Alamy/Juan Carlos Lino p**90** (Eufrasia); Corbis/Janet Jarman p**91** (Salvador); Getty Images/PhotoDisc p**96** (Carolina, Isabel); Robert Harding World Imagery/Michael Jenner p**97** (Bermeo harbour); Alamy/HEMIS p**97** (Mundaka beach); Digital Vision p**98** (plane); Getty Images/AFP p**122** (Gabriel García Márquez); Corbis/Reuters p**122** (Gabriel Batistuta). All other photographs were provided by Gareth Boden, Ben Nicholson, Jules Selmes and Pearson Education Ltd.

Every effort has been made to contact copyright holders of material reproduced in this book. Any omissions will be rectified in subsequent printings if notice is given to the publishers.

Contenidos

En la clase

During a task

I don't understand this.
What do I have to do?
You have to …
I need a dictionary.
This is (very) interesting.
This is (a bit) boring.
I need a tissue.
I need a pen/pencil.

Durante el ejercicio

No lo entiendo.
¿Qué hay que hacer?
Hay que …
Necesito un diccionario.
Esto es (muy) interesante.
Esto es (un poco) aburrido.
Necesito un pañuelo.
Necesito un boli/lápiz.

After a task

I've finished.
I haven't finished.
It was (very) difficult.
It was (quite) easy.
Can I go to the toilet?
I got everything right.
I made three mistakes.
What is the answer to number three?

Después del ejercicio

Ya he terminado.
Todavía no he terminado.
Era (muy) difícil.
Era (bastante) fácil.
¿Puedo ir al baño?
Tengo todo bien.
Cometí tres errores.
¿Cuál es la respuesta para el número tres?

Listening and reading

I understood everything.
I didn't understand anything.
Can we repeat number 4?
It is interesting.
It is boring.
It is too fast.
It is too long.

Escuchar y leer

Entendí todo.
No entendí nada.
¿Podemos repetir el número cuatro?
Es interesante.
Es aburrido.
Va demasiado rápido.
Es demasiado largo.

Speaking and writing

How do you spell …?
How do you say … in Spanish?
How do you pronounce this word?
I agree with you.
I don't agree with you.
Can you repeat the question?
Sorry, I don't know the answer.

Hablar y escribir

¿Cómo se escribe …?
¿Cómo se dice … en español?
¿Cómo se pronuncia esta palabra?
Estoy de acuerdo contigo.
No estoy de acuerdo contigo.
¿Puedes repetir la pregunta?
Lo siento, no sé la respuesta.

1 Mi ordenador

- Talking about what you use computers for
- Practising the present tense with frequency expressions

escuchar 1 Escucha y escribe la letra correcta.(1–8)

¿Qué haces con tu ordenador?

Ejemplo: **1** b

 **a** Leo y escribo correos.

b Descargo música.

 **c** Navego por internet.

 **d** Juego.

 **e** Chateo.

 **f** Hago mis deberes.

 **g** Veo DVDs.

 **h** Compro regalos.

escuchar 2 Escucha y escribe la letra correcta y la expresión de frecuencia. (1–8)

Ejemplo: **1** b, dos veces a la semana

todos los días
dos veces a la semana
los fines de semana
a veces
nunca

leer 3 Copia y completa el texto con el verbo correcto.

Ejemplo: **1** Juego

¡Hola! ¿Qué tal? Me llamo Jorge el Geek. Me encanta la tecnología.
(1) Juego / Escucho mucho con mi ordenador. Chateo todos los días. Los fines de semana leo y **(2) veo / escribo** correos.
(3) Hago / Juego mis deberes y **(4) descargo / navego** por internet un poco. También descargo música y **(5) leo / veo** DVDs.
A veces **(6) compro / chateo** regalos por internet pero este mes no tengo mucho dinero. ¡Qué lástima!

4 Escribe el verbo en español y en inglés.

Ejemplo: **1** compras   *you buy*

1 prascom	*you chat*
2 cargasdes	*you read*
3 teascha	*you see*
4 besescri	*you do*
5 slee	*you buy*
6 gasjue	*you download*
7 cesha	*you write*
8 sev	*you play*

Gramática

The present tense: regular verbs

	-ar verbs **comprar** (*to buy*)	**-er** verbs **leer** (*to read*)	**-ir** verbs **escribir** (*to write*)
(*I*) yo	compr**o**	le**o**	escrib**o**
(*you*) tú	compr**as**	le**es**	escrib**es**
(*he/she*) él/ella	compr**a**	le**e**	escrib**e**

Some verbs have an irregular 'I' form in the present tense:
hacer → yo hago (*I do/make*)

Some verbs change their stem:
jugar → yo juego (*I play*)

Para saber más   página 00

 5 Haz este quiz con tu compañero/a.

¿Qué haces con tu ordenador?

1 ¿Descargas música?
a Descargo música todos los días.
b Descargo música a veces.
c Nunca descargo música.

2 ¿Compras regalos?
a Compro regalos dos veces a la semana.
b Compro regalos a veces.
c Nunca compro regalos.

3 ¿Chateas?
a Chateo los fines de semana.
b Chateo a veces.
c Nunca chateo.

4 ¿Navegas por internet?
a Navego por internet todos los días.
b Navego por internet los fines de semana.
c Nunca navego por internet.

5 ¿Haces tus deberes?
a Hago mis deberes todos los días.
b Hago mis deberes a veces.
c Nunca hago mis deberes.

6 ¿Juegas?
a Juego todos los días.
b Juego dos veces a la semana.
c Nunca juego.

7 ¿Ves DVDs?
a Veo DVDs a veces.
b Veo DVDs los fines de semana.
c Nunca veo DVDs.

8 ¿Lees y escribes correos?
a Leo y escribo correos todos los días.
b Leo y escribo correos a veces.
c Nunca leo o escribo correos.

Tienes una mayoría de **a**:
Eres un geek. Pasas demasiado tiempo con el ordenador. Te encanta la informática pero mira, no olvides tus amigos …

Tienes una mayoría de **b**:
¡Felicidades! Tienes una vida equilibrada. Te gusta bastante tu ordenador, pero te encanta salir con tus amigos también.

Tienes una mayoría de **C**:
Por favor, conéctate. ¡Eres un Picapiedra! Tienes que decir 'hola' al mundo moderno.

 6 ¿Y tú? ¿Qué haces con tu ordenador?

Ejemplo: Con mi ordenador descargo música todos los días. También …

1 Escucha y escribe la letra correcta. (1–10)

a un programa de música

b un programa de deporte

c un programa de tele-realidad

d un concurso

e un documental

f una comedia

g una serie de policías

h una telenovela

i el telediario

j el tiempo

2 Escucha y escribe la letra correcta y el tipo de programa. (1–8)

Ejemplo: **1** b – programa de deporte

¿Cuál es tu programa favorito?

Mi programa favorito se llama …
Es un/una …

a Los Simpson	**e** Músicauno
b Territorio Champions	**f** Gran Hermano
c Andalucía es su nombre	**g** ¿Quién quiere ser millonario?
d Ley y orden	**h** Yo soy Bea

3 Con tu compañero/a, haz un diálogo.

● ¿Cuál es tu programa favorito?
■ Mi programa favorito es …
● Es un/una …

¿Quién quiere ser millonario?

Coronation Street

EastEnders

Little Britain

Doctor Who

4 Escucha y lee. Escribe los tipos de programas mencionados.

Ejemplo: 1 los programas de tele-realidad, las telenovelas

un rollo = *a drag*

Hola, me llamo Cintia. Me gustan los programas de tele-realidad porque son divertidos. Mi programa favorito es *Gran Hermano*. Pero no me gustan las telenovelas porque son tontas.

¿Qué tal? Me llamo Diego. Me encantan las series de policías porque son muy emocionantes. Mi programa favorito es *CSI Miami*. Pero no me gustan los concursos porque son aburridos.

¡Hola! Me llamo Ramón. Me gustan los documentales porque son informativos, pero no me gustan nada los programas de música porque no son interesantes. ¡*Músicauno* es muy aburrido!

Hola, soy Patricia. Me gustan mucho los programas de música porque son emocionantes y me gusta bailar, pero no me gustan los concursos porque son tontos. *¿Quién quiere ser millonario?* es un rollo.

5 Lee los textos otra vez. ¿Positivo o negativo? Copia y completa la tabla.

	fresco	fresquísimo	podrido	superpodrido
1	los programas de tele-realidad		las telenovelas	

Me gusta 🍅 Me encanta 🍅🍅 No me gusta No me gusta nada	**el** telediario **el** tiempo	porque es	emocionante interesante divertido informativo aburrido tonto
Me gusta**n** 🍅 Me encanta**n** 🍅🍅 No me gusta**n** No me gusta**n** nada	**los** programas de … **los** concursos **los** documentales **las** comedias **las** series de policías **las** telenovelas	porque **son**	emocionante**s** interesante**s** divertid**os/as** informativ**os/as** aburrid**os/as** tont**os/as**

6 Escribe un párrafo.

Ejemplo: Me encantan … porque son … Mi programa favorito es …
Pero no me gustan … porque son …

Talking about films
Using comparatives (**más … que**)

 1 **Escucha y escribe la letra correcta. (1–9)**

Ejemplo: **1** b

 *¿Qué tipo de películas te gustan?*

 **a**

las películas de amor

 **b**

las películas de acción

c

las películas de terror

 **d**

las películas de ciencia-ficción

 **e**

las películas de guerra

 **f**

las películas del Oeste

 **g**

las películas de artes marciales

h

las comedias

 **i**

los dibujos animados

 2 **Con tu compañero/a, haz diálogos.**

● ¿Qué tipo de películas prefieres?
■ Prefiero las películas de terror.

Gramática

Comparatives

más	+ adjective + **que**	*more … than*
menos	+ adjective + **que**	*less … than*

Para saber más página 00

 3 **Escucha y escribe la letra correcta. (1–4)**

Ejemplo: **1** b

↑ = más
↓ = menos

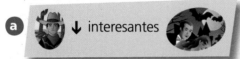 **a** ↓ interesantes

 b ↑ informativas

 **c** ↑ divertidas

 **d** ↓ aburridas

 4 **Empareja las frases con los dibujos correctos del ejercicio 3.**

Ejemplo: **1** b

1 Las películas de guerra son más informativas que las películas de artes marciales.

2 Las películas de acción son menos aburridas que las películas de ciencia-ficción.

3 Las películas del Oeste son menos interesantes que las películas de terror.

4 Las películas de terror son más divertidas que las películas de amor.

escribir 5 **Escribe tu opinión sobre estas películas.**

Ejemplo: **a** Las películas de artes marciales son más emocionante**s** que las películas de terror.

> Remember to change the endings of the adjectives to match the nouns they describe.

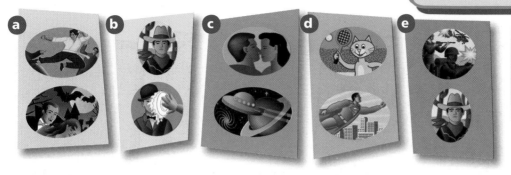

> emocionante
> interesante
> divertido
> informativo
> aburrido

escribir 6 **Copia el texto y escribe las palabras correctas.**

1

Me gusta mucho ir al cine pero también me gusta ver **(1)** ___ en casa. A veces descargo películas de internet. Me gustan mucho **(2)** ___ , pero no me gustan nada las películas del Oeste. **(3)** ___ son más emocionantes que otras películas. Daniel Craig es mi actor favorito. ¡Qué guapo es!

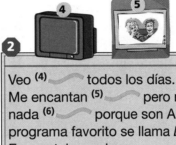

2

Veo **(4)** ___ todos los días. Me encantan **(5)** ___ pero no me gustan nada **(6)** ___ porque son ABURRIDAS. Mi programa favorito se llama *Dawson's Creek*. Es una telenovela. No me gusta mucho **(7)** ___ . Es un poco más interesante que el programa del tiempo, pero no mucho. Me gustan bastante **(8)** ___ porque me gusta escuchar música.

escribir 7 **Escribe un blog sobre las películas y los programas de televisión.**

- *Say how often you download films from the internet*
- *Say what type of films you like and why*
- *Say what your favourite TV programme is called*
- *Say why you like this type of programme*
- *Compare films and TV programmes using* **más … que**
- *Use connectives such as* **y**, **pero**, **o** *and* **también**

A veces descargo …
Me gustan … porque …
Mi programa favorito es …
Me gusta porque es …
Es más divertido que …
También me gusta …

Mini-test

I can
- say what I use computers for
- say how often I do things
- talk about television programmes and films
- give opinions and reasons
- **G** use comparatives
- **G** use the present tense

- Talking about different types of music
- Using the near future (**voy a ...**)

1 Escucha y escribe el tipo de música. (1–8)

Ejemplo: **1**, el jazz

a la música clásica
b la música latina
c la música electrónica
d el pop

e la música de los años sesenta
f el rock
g el rap
h el jazz

2 Escucha y escribe los datos en inglés. (1–6)

Ejemplo: **1** Likes rock. Doesn't like Latin music.

3 Con tu compañero/a, pregunta y contesta.

- ¿Qué tipo de música te gusta?
- Me encanta ..., me gusta ..., pero no me gusta nada ... y odio ...

Me encanta

Me gusta mucho

Me gusta

No me gusta

No me gusta nada

Odio

el pop, el rock, ...
la música clásica,
la música latina,
la música de los años 60,
...

 4 Empareja las frases de manera lógica.

Ejemplo: **1** Me gusta el rap.
d Mañana voy a ir a un concierto de Kanye West.

1 Me gusta el rap.
2 Me gusta el jazz.
3 Me gusta la música clásica.
4 Me gusta la música electrónica.
5 Me gusta el rock.

a Este fin de semana voy a ir a un concierto de Murray Perahia.
b Mañana voy a ir a un concierto de Amy Winehouse.
c Esta tarde voy a ir a un concierto de Franz Ferdinand.
d Mañana voy a ir a un concierto de Kanye West.
e Esta tarde voy a ir a un concierto de Hot Chip.

Murray Perahia

Amy Winehouse

Kanye West

Franz Ferdinand

Hot Chip

Gramática

The near future

ir *(to go)* + **a** + *infinitive*

(I)	voy a
(you)	vas a
(he/she/it)	va a
(we)	vamos a
(you pl.)	vais a
(they)	van a

Voy a ir a un concierto.
I'm going to go to a concert.

Vamos a ver una película.
We are going to see a film.

Para saber más   página 128; ej. 1

 5 Escucha y lee. Luego copia y rellena el perfil.

---

www.carolina.es

Hola. Me llamo Carolina. En mi tiempo libre leo y escribo correos. Navego mucho por internet todos los días. A veces hago mis deberes con mi ordenador.

También descargo música. Me gusta la música electrónica y el jazz. No me gusta nada la música clásica. Este fin de semana voy a ir a un concierto de Lily Allen. ¡Va a ser estupendo!

Me gusta ver la televisión. A veces veo documentales. Me gustan porque son informativos pero odio los programas de tele-realidad. Son aburridos.

Este fin de semana también voy a ver DVDs. Prefiero las películas de terror porque son divertidas. ¡Son más interesantes que las películas de amor! ¡Las pelis de amor son un rollo! También me gustan las películas de artes marciales. Mi actor favorito es Yun-Fat Chow.

---

www.carolina.es

Perfil

1 Nombre:
2 Tiempo libre:
3 ♥ Música:
4 ✗ Música:
5 Este fin de semana:
6 ♥ Televisión:
7 ✗ Televisión:
8 ♥ Películas:
9 ✗ Películas:

---

 6 Escucha y rellena el perfil del ejercicio 5 para Teo.

7 Escribe un blog sobre música. Utiliza el texto del ejercicio 5 como modelo.

escuchar 1 Escucha y lee.

El fin de semana pasado salí con mi hermana.

Fui a un concierto de los Arctic Monkeys.

Compré una camiseta …

Canté … y bailé …

Saqué fotos.

Fue estupendo.

Comí una pizza, ¡qué rica!

El domingo descargué el nuevo CD de los Arctic Monkeys.

leer 2 Busca estos verbos en español en el texto.

Ejemplo: **1** canté

1 I sang	**4** I went	**7** It was
2 I downloaded	**5** I bought	**8** I danced
3 I ate	**6** I went out	**9** I took

Gramática

The preterite tense

	-ar verbs **comprar** *(to buy)* *(bought)*	**-er** verbs **comer** *(to eat)* *(ate)*	**-ir** verbs **salir** *(to go out)* *(went out)*	**Irregular** verbs **ser/ir** *(to be/to go)* *(was, were/went)*
(I) yo	compr**é**	com**í**	sal**í**	fui
(you) tú	compr**aste**	com**iste**	sal**iste**	fu**iste**
(he/she) él/ella	compr**ó**	com**ió**	sal**ió**	fue

Para saber más

página 132

escuchar 3 Escucha y escribe las letras correctas. (1–4)

Ejemplo: **1** b, f, …

¿Adónde fuiste?
Fui a un concierto de …

a b c d

¿Con quién saliste?
Salí con …

e f g h

mis padres | mi hermano | mis hermanas

¿Qué hiciste?

i j k l

¿Qué comiste?
Comí …

m n o p

¿Qué tal lo pasaste?
Lo pasé …

q r s t

hablar 4 Con tu compañero/a, haz dos diálogos utilizando el ejercicio 3.

leer 5 Lee los textos y escribe cinco datos en inglés sobre cada texto.

Ejemplo: Dolores: last weekend, …

El fin de semana pasado fui a un concierto de Avril Lavigne en Madrid. Fue emocionante. Después fui a un restaurante con mis amigos. Comí pollo con patatas fritas. ¡Qué rico!
Dolores

Ayer salí con mi hermana. Fui a un concierto de rock pero no fue interesante. Luego fui a una cafetería y después a la discoteca. Bailé mucho. ¡Fue guay!
Javier

escribir 6 Describe un concierto.

Fui a un concierto de …

Salí con …

Canté …/Bailé …/Compré …/Saqué …

Fue …

Comí …

Remember to use time expressions when you talk about past events:

La semana pasada	*Last week*
El fin de semana pasado	*Last weekend*
El viernes pasado	*Last Friday*
Ayer	*Yesterday*

Resumen

Unidad 1

I can

- talk about what I use my computer for

  Leo y escribo correos. Descargo música. Navego por internet.

- ask someone what they do with their computer

  ¿Qué haces con tu ordenador?

- use expressions of frequency

  todos los días, dos veces a la semana, a veces

- use the **tú** form of verbs to ask questions

  ¿Chateas por internet? ¿Compras regalos?

- G use the present tense of different types of verbs

  Navego por internet. ¿**Lees** y **escribes** correos? **Hago** mis deberes.

Unidad 2

I can

- name types of television programmes

  un concurso, un programa de deporte, el telediario

- ask someone about their favourite TV programme

  ¿Cuál es tu programa favorito?

- talk about my favourite programme

  Mi programa favorito es EastEnders. Es una telenovela.

- give opinions and reasons

  Me gustan mucho los programas de deporte porque son emocionantes.

Unidad 3

I can

- name different types of films

  las películas de guerra, las películas de amor, las comedias

- ask someone what sort of films they prefer

  ¿Qué tipo de películas prefieres?

- give opinions on types of films

  Me gustan las películas de guerra porque son divertidas e informativas.

- G use comparatives

  Las películas de terror son **más** emocionantes **que** las películas de amor.

Unidad 4

I can

- talk about what type of music I like

  Me gusta la música clásica. No me gusta el rock.

- ask someone what type of music they like

  ¿Qué tipo de música te gusta?

- G use the near future tense

  Este fin de semana voy a ir a un concierto de jazz.

- G write sentences in the present and near future tenses

  En mi tiempo libre navego por internet. Esta tarde voy a ir a un concierto.

Unidad 5

I can

- use past time expressions

  ayer ..., el viernes pasado ..., anteayer ...

- G use the preterite (simple past) tense

  Ayer salí con mi hermana. Fui a la discoteca. Bailé mucho.

1 Escucha y contesta a las preguntas para cada persona. (1–3)

Ejemplo: **1 a** Veo DVDs.

a ¿Qué haces con tu ordenador?
b ¿Qué tipo de música te gusta?
c ¿Qué tipo de películas prefieres?
d ¿Por qué?
e ¿Cuál es tu programa favorito?

2 Con tu compañero/a, haz un diálogo.

- ¿Qué haces con tu ordenador?
- ¿Qué tipo de música te gusta?
- ¿Qué tipo de películas prefieres?
- ¿Por qué?
- ¿Cuál es tu programa favorito?

- Normalmente …
- Me gusta …
- Prefiero …
- Porque …
- Mi programa favorito es …

3 Lee el texto. Contesta a las preguntas en inglés.

Ejemplo: **1** Eva surfs the net every day.

Eva

Navego por internet todos los días. Leo y escribo correos
a mis amigos. Pero nunca voy de compras.
A veces descargo música. Me encanta la música latina y la música clásica,
pero no me gusta nada el rock.
En mi tiempo libre veo películas. Me encantan las comedias porque son
divertidas. Son más interesantes que las películas de acción.
También veo la tele. Me encantan las telenovelas, pero no me gustan nada
los programas de deportes porque son un rollo.

1 How often does Eva use the internet?
2 What does she sometimes do?
3 What does she never do?
4 What types of music does she like and dislike?
5 What type of films does she prefer and why?
6 What type of TV programmes does she like and dislike?

4 Escribe un párrafo sobre un concierto.

Ejemplo: Ayer salí con mi hermano …

Ayer salí con …
Fui a …
Fue …
Bailé …
Fui a …
Comí …

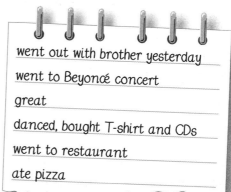

went out with brother yesterday
went to Beyoncé concert
great
danced, bought T-shirt and CDs
went to restaurant
ate pizza

Escucha y lee.

El flamenco

gitano = *gypsy*
profundo = *deep*

El flamenco es un arte muy antiguo que nació en el sur de España, en Andalucía. Este estilo musical también se llama arte gitano y tiene tres elementos básicos: el cante, el baile y la guitarra. El cante más antiguo se llama cante Jondo, o profundo. Es un estilo serio y trágico. Pero también existe el flamenco Festero, que es más divertido y además es muy popular en las fiestas de Andalucía.

Escucha y lee. Luego contesta a las preguntas en inglés.

www.ojosdebrujo.com

Ojos de Brujo

estilos = *styles*
grabó = *recorded*
tocó = *played*

Ojos de Brujo es un grupo de música de Barcelona. Su música es una fusión de varios estilos, como el flamenco, el reggae, el hip-hop, el rock y la música electrónica.
En 1999, Ojos de Brujo grabó su primer álbum *Vengue*.
En 2002 salió su segundo álbum *Barí*. Ojos de Brujo tocó en los festivales más importantes de jazz, rock y world music.
El 20 de febrero de 2006 publicaron *Techarí*, su tercer álbum, de flamenco experimental.

1　Where does the group come from?
2　What different styles of music are in their songs?
3　When did they record their first album?
4　What is their second album called?
5　Which festivals have they played at?
6　Describe their third album.

 Con tu compañero/a, escucha y luego da tu opinión de la música de Ojos de Brujo.

● ¿Te gusta la música de Ojos de Brujo?
■ Sí, me gusta./No. No me gusta.

porque es / porque no es … … y / pero / también es	muy / bastante / un poco seria / divertida / trágica / alegre / buena / mala / aburrida / guay
Hay elementos	del reggae / hip-hop / rock / flamenco. de la música electrónica.

4 Escribe un artículo sobre un grupo de música.

> ... es un grupo de música de ...
> Su música es una fusión de ... y ...
> En ... grabaron su primer álbum ...
> En ... salió su segundo álbum ...
> Tocaron en los festivales de ...
> En ... publicaron ..., su tercer álbum ...
> Me gusta la música de ... porque es ...

5 Escucha y canta.

En el karaoke canta Katarina
pero, como siempre, ella desafina.
Ópera, jazz ... ¡da igual!
Rock, pop ... ¡canta fatal!

desafina = *sings out of tune*
¡da igual! = *it doesn't matter*
bailarina = *dancer*
orquesta = *orchestra*

En la discoteca baila Katarina
pero ella no es una bailarina.
Tango, flamenco ... ¡da igual!
Salsa, hip-hop ... ¡baila fatal!

Ayer tocó la flauta en la orquesta
pero cuando tocó, ¡adiós a la fiesta!
Guitarra, trompeta ... ¡da igual!
Flauta, violín ... ¡toca fatal!

Va a trabajar en un musical.
Va a ser Mary Poppins, ¡ay, qué mal!
Cantar, bailar, tocar ... ¡da igual!
Porque todo, todo ... ¡lo hace fatal!

6 Contesta a las preguntas en inglés.

1 Find the Spanish for:
  a four musical instruments
  b four types of music
  c four types of dance.

2 'Baila fatal' means 'she dances terribly'. Can you translate the following:
  a toca fatal
  b canta fatal

Gramática

1 **Which is the odd one out? Give a reason why.**

Example: **1** c, because *escribo* is the only -ir verb

1 **a** Compro regalos. **b** Descargo música. **c** Escribo correos.

2 **a** Navego por internet. **b** Hago mis deberes. **c** Chateo.

3 **a** ¿Descargas música? **b** ¿Lees correos? **c** ¿Chateas?

4 **a** Compra regalos. **b** Juega. **c** Veo DVDs.

5 **a** Juegas. **b** Navego por internet. **c** Chateas.

6 **a** Navegar. **b** Descargar. **c** Leo.

2 **Choose the correct option to complete the sentences.**

Example: **1** favorito

1 Mi programa **favorito / favorita** es *¿Quién quiere ser millonario?*.
2 También me gustan los programas de tele-realidad porque son **divertido / divertidos**.
3 No me gustan nada las telenovelas porque son **tontos / tontas**.
4 Las telenovelas no son **informativa / informativas**.
5 Me gusta el telediario porque es informativo e **interesante / interesantes**.
6 No me gusta el tiempo – es muy **aburrido / aburrida**.

3 **Antonio has spilt Coke all over his adjective endings. Write them out correctly for him.**

1 Me gustan mucho los programas de deporte – no son aburrid⬛⬛.
2 Las telenovelas son muy interesant⬛⬛, pero no me gustan nada.
3 Las telenovelas no son emocionant⬛⬛.
4 Las telenovelas son muy aburrid⬛⬛.
5 Me encantan los documentales porque son muy informativ⬛⬛.
6 Los documentales son interesant⬛⬛ también.
7 Me gustan los dibujos animados porque son divertid⬛⬛.
8 No me gusta el programa del tiempo – no es nada interesant⬛⬛.

4 **Write out these sentences in a logical order, then translate them into English.**

Example: **1** Las películas del Oeste son más divertidas que las comedias.
Westerns are funnier than comedies.

1 que las comedias / del Oeste / Las películas / son / más divertidas
2 de artes marciales / de ciencia-ficción / Las películas / más emocionantes / son / que las películas
3 de amor / de acción / son / que / las películas / Las películas / más interesantes
4 de ciencia-ficción / menos informativos / Los dibujos animados / son / que / las películas
5 de amor / Las películas / son / que / las películas / de terror / menos aburridas

5 Using the verb box and the words below to help you, translate these sentences into Spanish.

Example: **1** Voy a salir con mi hermana.

① I am going to go out with my sister.
② I am going to buy a T-shirt.
③ I am going to sing a lot.
④ I am going to take photos.
⑤ I am going to download music.
⑥ I am going to eat chips.
⑦ I am going to dance with my brother.
⑧ I am going to go to a concert.

Voy a	ir
	comer
	descargar
	comprar
	sacar
	salir
	bailar
	cantar

a un concierto   fotos   una camiseta   con mi hermano

música   mucho   patatas fritas   con mi hermana

 6 Write the English for all the highlighted verbs in these sentences. Then match up the correct pictures to the sentences.

Example: fui   *I went*

① El fin de semana pasado **fui** a un concierto de jazz con mi hermano. **Fue** genial.
② Ayer **compré** un CD de Justin Timberlake y **fui** a su concierto en Barcelona. ¡**Fue** guay!
③ La semana pasada **fui** a un concierto de R. Kelly. Después **comí** patatas fritas. **Fue** genial.
④ Ayer **fui** a un concierto de mi grupo favorito, **compré** una camiseta y **saqué** muchas fotos. Después, me **descargué** su nuevo álbum.
⑤ El fin de semana pasado **salí** con mi hermana. **Fui** a un concierto de Britney Spears. **Canté** y **bailé**. Después **fui** a una cafetería y **comí** churros.

Palabras

Mi ordenador
¿Qué haces con tu ordenador?
Leo y escribo correos.
Descargo música.
Navego por internet.
Juego.
Chateo.
Hago mis deberes.
Veo DVDs.
Compro regalos.
todos los días
dos veces a la semana
los fines de semana
a veces
nunca

The computer
What do you do with your computer?
I read and write emails.
I download music.
I surf the net.
I play games.
I chat online.
I do my homework.
I watch DVDs.
I buy presents.
every day
twice a week
at weekends
sometimes
never

La televisión
¿Cuál es tu programa favorito?

Mi programa favorito es …
Es …
un concurso
un documental
un programa de deporte
un programa de música
un programa de tele-realidad
el telediario
el tiempo
una comedia
una serie de policías
una telenovela

Television
What's your favourite television programme?

My favourite programme is …
It's …
a game show
a documentary
a sports show

a music show

a reality show

the news
the weather
a comedy
a detective series
a soap opera

¿Por qué te gusta?
Me gusta/Me gustan …
Me encanta/Me encantan …
No me gusta/No me gustan …
porque es …
porque son …
aburridos/as
divertidos/as
emocionantes
informativos/as
interesantes
malos/as
tontos/as
un rollo

Why do you like it?
I like …

I love …

I don't like …

because it is …
because they are …
boring
entertaining
moving
informative
interesting
bad
stupid
a drag

Las películas
¿Qué tipo de películas te gustan?
Me gustan …
Prefiero …
las películas de …
acción
amor
artes marciales
ciencia-ficción
guerra
terror
las películas del Oeste
las comedias
los dibujos animados

Films
What sort of films do you like?
I like …
I prefer …
… films
action
romantic
martial arts
sci-fi
war
horror
Westerns
comedies
cartoons/animations

Más o menos
más … que
menos … que
Los dibujos animados son más divertidos que las películas de terror.
Las comedias son menos interesantes que las películas del Oeste.

More or less
more … than
less … than
Cartoons are funnier than horror films.

Comedies are less interesting than Westerns.

La música	Music
la música clásica	classical music
la música de los años sesenta	sixties music
la música electrónica	electronic music
la música latina	Latin music
la música pop	pop music
el jazz	jazz
el rap	rap
el rock	rock
¿Qué tipo de música te gusta?	What sort of music do you like?
Me encanta la música pop.	I love pop music.
Me gusta mucho el rap.	I really like rap.
Me gusta el jazz.	I like jazz.
No me gusta la música latina.	I don't like Latin music.
No me gusta nada el rock.	I don't like rock at all.
Odio la música clásica.	I hate classical music.

Fui a un concierto …	I went to a concert …
¿Adónde fuiste?	Where did you go?
Fui a un concierto de Shakira.	I went to a Shakira concert.
¿Con quién saliste?	Who did you go out with?
Salí con …	I went out with …
¿Qué hiciste …?	What did you do …?
Canté.	I sang.
Bailé.	I danced.
Compré una camiseta.	I bought a T-shirt.
Saqué fotos.	I took photos.
¿Qué comiste?	What did you eat?
Comí una pizza.	I ate a pizza.
¿Cómo fue?	How was it?
Fue …	It was …
estupendo	fantastic
guay	cool
aburrido	boring
un desastre	a disaster
ayer	yesterday

el viernes pasado	last Friday
la semana pasada	last week
el fin de semana pasado	last weekend

Palabras muy útiles	Very useful words
y	and
pero	but
o	or
también	also, as well
primero	first
luego	then
después	afterwards

Estrategia

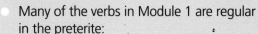

Using the preterite

- Many of the verbs in Module 1 are regular in the preterite:
  escuchar (to listen)   escuché (I listened)
  comer (to eat)   comí (I ate)
  salir (to go out)   salí (I went out)

- You've also met some verbs that are irregular:
  ser (to be)   fui (I was)
  ir (to go)   fui (I went)

  Often, the irregular verbs don't have the accents that regular ones do.

Try writing these verbs out on sticky notes and sticking them on your diary, around your bedroom or on the fridge, so that you see them often and learn them.

1 Un día en el instituto

○ Describing your school
● Asking and answering
questions about school

 1 Escucha y lee. Empareja las frases con los dibujos. (1–6)

Ejemplo: **1** e

a

b

c

d

e

f

1 Mi instituto se llama Instituto Antonio Machado.
2 Hay mil alumnos.
3 Hay setenta y cinco profesores.

4 Hay cinco clases al día.
5 No llevo uniforme.
6 Me gusta mucho mi instituto.

 2 Lee las preguntas y busca estas palabras en español.

Ejemplo: **a** *your school* – tu instituto

1 ¿Cómo se llama tu instituto? **a** *your school*
2 ¿Cuántos alumnos hay? **d** *pupils*
3 ¿Cuántos profesores hay? **e** *teachers*
4 ¿Cuántas clases hay al día? **b** *lessons*
5 ¿Llevas uniforme? **c** *uniform*
6 ¿Te gusta tu instituto?

Gramática

Asking questions

You can make questions with question words:
¿Cómo? *What? How?*
¿Cuántos? ¿Cuántas? *How many?*

Questions can also be made without question words, but with rising intonation:

¿Llevas uniforme? → *Do you wear uniform?*

Remember that verb endings change in questions and answers:
¿Llev**as** uniforme? → Llev**o** uniforme.

Other words also change:
¿**Te** gusta **tu** instituto? → **Me** gusta **mi** instituto.

Para saber más página 000

 3 Escucha. Copia y rellena la tabla en inglés.

1 Name of school	Manuel de Falla
2 Pupils?	
3 Teachers?	
4 Lessons per day?	
5 Uniform?	
6 ♥ ✗	

4 Con tu compañero/a, haz un diálogo sobre tu instituto. Utiliza las preguntas del ejercicio 2.

● ¿Cómo se llama tu instituto?
■ Mi instituto se llama <u>Greenbank School</u>.

5 Escucha. Escribe el día y la letra correcta. (1–9)

Ejemplo: **1** Fridays, c

¿Qué haces en el recreo?
Los lunes …   Los jueves …
Los martes …   Los viernes …
Los miércoles …

o = *or*

a
Voy al club de teatro.

b
Voy al club de informática.

c
Voy al club de ajedrez.

d
Voy al patio.

e
Voy a la cantina.

f
Toco en la orquesta.

g
Voy a la biblioteca.

h
Juego al fútbol.

i
Canto en el coro.

6 Escribe tus actividades de cada día, luego, con tu compañero/a, haz un diálogo.

● ¿Qué haces los <u>lunes</u> en el recreo?
■ Los <u>lunes</u>, <u>voy al club de teatro</u> …

Los lunes … club de teatro
Los martes … fútbol

7 Escribe un blog sobre tu instituto. Utiliza las frases de Teo como modelo.

www.teo.es

Mi instituto se llama Camden School.
Hay … alumnos.
Hay … profesores.
Hay … clases al día.
(No) Llevo uniforme.
(No) Me gusta mucho mi instituto.
Los lunes, en el recreo, voy al / a la …
Los martes …

Perfil
Nombre: Teo

2 ¿Qué vas a estudiar?

 1 Escucha y escribe la letra de la asignatura. (1–12)

a el español
b el francés
c el inglés
d el diseño
e el comercio
f el dibujo
g el teatro
h la historia
i la música
j la informática
k la geografía
l la educación física
m la tecnología
n las ciencias
o las matemáticas

2 Escucha otra vez y escribe la opinión en inglés.

Ejemplo: **1** Likes science – interesting

Estudio matemáticas.	*I study maths.*
Me gusta**n las** matemáticas.	*I like maths.*
Estudio francés.	*I study French.*
Me gusta **el** francés.	*I like French.*

el + *subject*	la + *subject*	las +
aburrid**o**	aburrid**a**	aburrid**as**
creativ**o**	creativ**a**	creativ**as**
divertid**o**	divertid**a**	divertid**as**
interesante		interesante**s**
importante		importante**s**
difícil		difícil**es**
fácil		fácil**es**
útil		útil**es**
guay		guay

> Make sure you stress accented letters. Listen and repeat these words: difícil, difíciles, fácil, fáciles, útil, útiles

 3 Con tu compañero/a, haz cinco diálogos.
Cambia las asignaturas y las opiniones subrayadas.

- ¿Qué estudias?
- Estudio <u>inglés</u>.
- ¿Te gusta?
- <u>No, no me gusta nada el inglés</u>.
- ¿Por qué?
- Porque es <u>aburrido</u>.

- ¿Qué estudias?
- Estudio <u>ciencias</u>.
- ¿Te gusta**n**?
- <u>Sí, me gusta**n** mucho las ciencias</u>.
- ¿Por qué?
- Porque <u>son divertid**as**</u>.

Lee los textos.
Copia y rellena la tabla en inglés.

Name	Subject	Opinion
Antonio	science	interesting not difficult

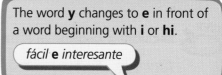
The word **y** changes to **e** in front of a word beginning with **i** or **hi**.

*fácil **e** interesante*

además = *also*

El año que viene voy a estudiar ciencias. Me gustan porque son muy interesantes y no son difíciles. ¡Me encanta hacer experimentos en el laboratorio!

Antonio

El año que viene voy a estudiar dibujo. Me encanta el dibujo porque es fácil y además es muy creativo.

Carol

El año que viene voy a estudiar comercio y diseño. Me gusta el comercio porque es divertido y el diseño porque es guay.

Rico

El año que viene no voy a estudiar educación física. No me gusta nada hacer ejercicio. ¡Es un rollo!

Cintia

 Escucha y escribe la asignatura y la opinión. (1–5)

Ejemplo: **1** geography, useful

easy	not boring	cool	important

useful	creative	interesting

Gramática

Present	Near future
Estudio …	Voy a estudiar …
I study …	*I am going to study …*

Use time phrases about the future too:
El año que viene … *Next year …*

Para saber más página 00

 Con tu compañero/a, haz un diálogo.

● ¿Qué vas a estudiar el año que viene?
■ El año que viene voy a estudiar …
● ¿Por qué te gusta …?/¿Por qué te gustan …?
■ Porque es … /Porque son …

Escribe un texto sobre el año que viene. Utiliza los textos del ejercicio 4 como modelos.

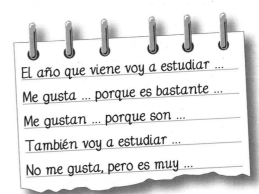

El año que viene voy a estudiar …
Me gusta … porque es bastante …
Me gustan … porque son …
También voy a estudiar …
No me gusta, pero es muy …

3 Se debe . . .

● Talking about school rules
● Using **se debe** to say 'you must …'

1 Escucha y escribe la letra correcta. (1–10)

Ejemplo: **1** e

Las normas del instituto

a Se debe escuchar en clase.

b Se debe hacer los deberes.

c Se debe llevar uniforme.

d Se debe llegar a tiempo.

e No se debe llevar zapatillas de deporte.

f No se debe llevar joyas.

g No se debe llevar maquillaje.

h No se debe comer chicle.

i No se debe correr en los pasillos.

j No se debe usar el móvil en clase.

2 Juego de memoria.

● No se debe usar el móvil en clase.
■ No se debe usar el móvil en clase.
No se debe llevar joyas …

> " Listen and make sure you know how to pronounce the letters **z**, **j** and **ll** in Spanish. Practise these sentences. "

*No se debe **ll**evar **z**apatillas de deporte.*

*No se debe **ll**evar **j**oyas.*

Gramática

Se debe + infinitive

Se debe means *you must*, referring to people in general. It is followed by an infinitive.

Se debe llevar uniforme.
You must wear uniform.

No se debe llevar joyas.
You must not wear jewellery.

Para saber más   página 00

3 Escucha y escribe las letras del ejercicio 1. (1–5)

Ejemplo: **1** i

 4 Empareja las descripciones con los dibujos.

1 En mi instituto se debe llevar zapatillas de deporte, se debe comer chicle, se debe llevar joyas y se debe usar el móvil en clase.

3 En mi instituto se debe escuchar en clase y se debe hacer los deberes. Eso es muy importante. Además se debe llegar a tiempo.

2 En mi instituto no se debe llevar uniforme. Se debe llevar joyas y se debe llevar maquillaje pero se debe escuchar en clase.

4 En mi instituto se debe correr por los pasillos y se debe llevar zapatillas de deporte. No se debe comer chicle y no se debe llevar joyas.

El instituto de los modelos

El instituto de los deportistas

El instituto de los empollones

El instituto de los raperos

 5 Escribe un blog y habla de las normas de un instituto imaginario.

Me gusta mucho mi instituto.
No se debe llevar uniforme pero se debe llegar a tiempo …

Mini-test

I can

- describe my school
- talk about after-school clubs
- say what I think of school subjects and why
- say what I am going to study next year
- talk about school rules
- **G** ask and answer different types of questions

4 Timoteo el travieso

escuchar 1 Escucha y lee.
¿Qué hizo ayer? ¿Qué no hizo? Haz una lista.

hizo = *he did*
ayer = *yesterday*
se enfadó mucho = *got really angry*

1 No me gusta el instituto.
Es muy aburrido.
Ayer llegué un poco tarde,
a las once de la mañana.

2 No escuché al profesor de
inglés pero escuché un
poco de música. Me gusta
la música electrónica.

3 En el recreo salí y me compré
un chicle. También comí dos
hamburguesas con patatas fritas. Bebí
una lata de Coca-Cola. ¡Qué rica!

4 Más tarde, en la clase de español,
mandé mensajes a mis amigos
y saqué fotos con mi móvil. Mi
profesor se enfadó mucho.

5 Luego hablé con mi hermano
por teléfono en la clase de
ciencias. No estudié mucho.
No me gustan las ciencias.

6 Después del colegio
jugué al voleibol en el
patio con mis amigos.

leer 2 Lee el texto otra vez y completa estas frases en inglés.

Ejemplo: **1** Timoteo arrived at 11 a.m.

1 Timoteo arrived at …
2 In his English lesson, he …
3 For lunch, he …
4 In his Spanish lesson he …
5 In his science lesson he …
6 After school he …

> Timoteo uses sequencers
> to structure his text:
>
> Más tarde   *later on*
> Luego   *later*
> Después   *afterwards*

leer 3 Busca estos verbos en español en el texto.

Ejemplo: **1** salí

1 I went out
2 I arrived
3 I sent
4 I listened
5 I bought
6 I studied
7 I ate
8 I took
9 I spoke
10 I played
11 I drank

Gramática

Regular verbs in the preterite

-ar verbs		**-er** verbs		**-ir** verbs	
hablar	*(to speak)*	**comer**	*(to eat)*	**salir**	*(to go out)*
hablé	*I spoke*	comí	*I ate*	salí	*I went out*
hablaste	*you spoke*	comiste	*you ate*	saliste	*you went out*
habló	*he/she spoke*	comió	*he/she ate*	salió	*he/she went out*

Some verbs have a small irregularity in the first person of the preterite:

jugar	*(to play)*	llegar	*(to arrive)*	sacar	*(to take – photos)*
jug**ué**	*I played*	lleg**ué**	*I arrived*	sa**qué**	*I took*

Para saber más.   página 00

4 Escucha y escribe los datos en inglés.

Ejemplo: **1** arrived at 12

1 Arrived at … Bought … Ate … Drank … Played …	**2** Didn't … in maths. Listened to … Sent texts to … Took … The teacher …

5 Con tu compañero/a, haz este quiz.

QUIZ

1 ¿Te gusta el instituto?
  a Sí, me gusta mucho.
  b Sí, me gusta bastante.
  c No, no me gusta nada. Es muy aburrido.

2 ¿A qué hora llegaste ayer?
  a Llegué a tiempo.
  b Llegué un poco tarde.
  c Llegué a las once de la mañana.

3 ¿Qué hiciste en el recreo?
  a Comí en la cantina.
  b Salí y compré fruta.
  c Salí y compré una hamburguesa con patatas fritas.

4 ¿Qué hiciste en la clase de matemáticas?
  a Escuché al profesor.
  b Escuché un poco de música pero trabajé mucho.
  c No escuché al profesor.

Si tienes una mayoría de:

a te gusta el instituto y trabajas bastante. Las asignaturas son interesantes para ti y te gustan tus profesores.

b te gusta bastante el instituto. Te gusta ver a tus amigos y pasar tiempo con ellos durante el recreo y después del colegio. A veces los profesores son un poco aburridos pero por lo general todo está bien.

c no te gusta nada el instituto. Prefieres escuchar música, mandar mensajes o hablar con tus amigos. Cuidado, amigo …

¿qué hiciste? = *what did you do?*
cuidado, amigo = *be careful my friend*

6 ¿Y tú? ¿Qué hiciste ayer?

Llegué a las …
En la clase de …
Luego en la clase de …
En el recreo salí y compré …
Más tarde en la clase de …
Después del colegio …

After you've finished, make sure you check for missing accents

- on your preterite verbs
- on your sequencers (*más tarde/ después …*)

Loli la traviesa

Writing a detailed description of your school
Using the present and preterite tenses together

 1 Escucha y lee. Luego responde a las preguntas en inglés.

Ejemplo: **1** 900 pupils

Mi instituto se llama Instituto Santa Marta. Hay novecientos alumnos y cincuenta profesores. No tengo que llevar uniforme.

Los lunes, en el recreo, voy a la biblioteca y los martes voy al club de informática. Me encanta la informática. Juego con el ordenador todos los días.

Tengo seis clases al día. Estudio inglés, matemáticas, ciencias, historia, geografía, tecnología, teatro, música y español. Me gustan las ciencias porque son interesantes. Pero no me gusta mucho el inglés porque es un poco aburrido y además es muy difícil.

En mi instituto no se debe comer chicle y no se debe correr en los pasillos. Se debe escuchar en clase y llegar a tiempo.

José

además = *also*

1 How many pupils are there at José's school?
2 How many teachers are there?
3 Does José wear uniform?
4 What does he do at breaktime on Mondays?
5 And on Tuesdays?
6 How many lessons are there each day?
7 Which subjects does José study?
8 What does he like?
9 What does he dislike?
10 Which rules does José mention?

 2 Escucha y lee. Luego termina las frases en inglés.

1 Yesterday, Alejandro arrived at …
2 He played …
3 In his English class, he …
4 During break, he …
5 In his Spanish class …
6 At lunchtime …
7 Later, in music …
8 After school …

¿Cómo es un día típico en mi instituto?
Ayer llegué a las ocho y jugué al fútbol en el patio con mis amigos. En la clase de inglés escuché y hablé. Leí y escribí. Trabajé mucho. En el recreo fui a la biblioteca. Luego en la clase de español, escuché al profesor y estudié mucho. En la hora de comer fui a casa.
Más tarde en la clase de música toqué la trompeta. Después del colegio, canté en el coro.

Look carefully at verb endings to check whether they are in the present or the preterite.

	-ar	-er	-ir
Present	escucho *(I listen)*	como *(I eat)*	escribo *(I write)*
Preterite	escuché *(I listened)*	comí *(I ate)*	escribí *(I wrote)*

Use context or time expressions to work out which tense is being used.

Los martes voy al club de informática.   *On Tuesdays I go to the ICT club.*
Ayer fui a la biblioteca.   *Yesterday I went to the library.*

3 Busca estos verbos en español en los textos de los ejercicios 1 y 2.

Ejemplo: **1** No tengo que llevar

1 I don't have to wear	**2** I go	**3** I love	**4** I study
5 I arrived	**6** I played (football)	**7** I listened	**8** I wrote

 4 Escucha. Copia y rellena la tabla. (1–8)

Normalmente	
Ayer	C, ...

 5 Prepárate. Luego, con tu compañero/a habla de tu instituto.

1 Los lunes, en el recreo …

2 Los jueves …

3 A veces, …

4 Ayer, …

5 Ayer, en la hora de comer …

6 Ayer, después del colegio …

6 Describe tu instituto.

Mi instituto se llama …	Me gusta mucho … porque es …
Hay … alumnos.	No me gusta mucho … porque es …
Hay … profesores.	En mi instituto no se debe …
Los lunes, en el recreo …	Ayer en la clase de …
Los martes …	Ayer en el recreo …
Hay … clases al día.	Ayer en la hora de comer …
Estudio …	Más tarde en la clase de …

Resumen

Unidad 1

I can

- ask someone questions about their school

  ¿Cómo se llama tu instituto?
  ¿Cuántos alumnos hay?

- describe my school

  Mi instituto se llama Instituto Antonio Machado.
  Hay cinco clases al día.

- talk about after-school clubs and activities

  Voy al club de informática.
  Canto en el coro. Juego al fútbol.

- **G** ask questions about school

  ¿Cómo se llama tu instituto?
  ¿Llevas uniforme?

Unidad 2

I can

- say what I study

  Estudio educación física.

- say what I think of school subjects and why

  Me gustan las ciencias porque son interesantes.

- say what I am going to study next year

  El año que viene voy a estudiar informática.

- **G** use adjectives to give opinions

  El dibujo es aburrido. Las ciencias son útiles.

Unidad 3

I can

- talk about school rules

  Se debe escuchar en clase.
  No se debe correr en los pasillos.

- use the impersonal verb **se debe**

  Se debe llegar a tiempo.

Unidad 4

I can

- talk about a day at school in the past

  Llegué a las once. Escuché música.

- use time expressions

  En el recreo salí y me compré un chicle. Más tarde en la clase de español, mandé mensajes a mis amigos. Después del colegio jugué al voleibol.

- **G** use the preterite

  llegué, escuché, salí, compré, jugué

Unidad 5

I can

- talk about what I do every day

  No llevo uniforme. Voy al club de informática.

- talk about a day in the past

  Ayer jugué al fútbol. En el recreo fui a la biblioteca.

- **G** distinguish between verbs in the present and preterite tenses

  escucho/escuché, como/comí

- **G** use time expressions to refer to the present and past

  Los lunes …, Normalmente …, Ayer …

1 Escucha y pon los dibujos en el orden correcto. (1–9)

Ejemplo: b, …

2 Con tu compañero/a, pregunta y contesta.

- ¿Cómo se llama tu instituto?
- ¿Cuántos alumnos hay?
- ¿Qué estudias?
- ¿Qué haces en el recreo?
- ¿Qué vas a estudiar el año que viene?

- Mi instituto se llama …
- Hay …
- Estudio …
- En el recreo …
- Voy a estudiar …

3 Lee el texto. Pon las normas en el orden correcto.

Ejemplo: **c**, …

En mi instituto hay mil alumnos y ochenta profesores. Me gusta mucho mi instituto, pero hay muchas normas. No se debe llevar zapatillas de deporte, por ejemplo. Y se debe llevar uniforme. No se debe llevar joyas y no se debe comer chicle. Finalmente, no se debe llevar maquillaje y no se debe usar el móvil en clase.

4 Escribe un párrafo sobre tus actividades extraescolares.

Presente	Pretérito
	Ayer en el recreo
Todos los días.	Después del colegio
Normalmente los viernes	

1 Escucha y empareja las fechas con las fiestas. (1–6)

Ejemplo: **1** d

1 de enero   **6 de enero**   **19 y 20 de febrero**   **marzo/abril**   **junio – septiembre**   **diciembre**

a Pascua y la Semana Santa	**d** el Año Nuevo
b el Día de los Reyes Magos	**e** las vacaciones de verano
c la Navidad	**f** el Carnaval

2 Escucha y lee el texto. Luego empareja el español y el inglés.

Ejemplo: **1** f

1 Nochebuena	**a** Christmas tree
2 ternera asada	**b** Christmas dinner
3 la cena navideña	**c** they leave presents
4 pavo	**d** roast beef
5 los Reyes Magos	**e** Christmas pudding
6 traen regalos	**f** Christmas Eve
7 un pudín de Navidad	**g** the Three Wise Men
8 el árbol de Navidad	**h** turkey

belén = *crib, nativity scene*
carbón = *coal*

Me llamo Juanita. La Navidad es una fiesta muy importante para mi familia.
En mi casa normalmente decoramos el árbol de Navidad y ponemos un belén. La casa está muy bonita con guirnaldas y luces.
En Nochebuena ceno ternera asada y en la cena navideña del día 25 como pavo y bebo cava, que es un tipo de champán.
El día 6 de enero es importante. Es el día de los Reyes Magos.
Los Reyes traen regalos a los niños buenos y a los niños malos … ¡carbón!
El año pasado en Navidades fui a Santa Cruz de Tenerife. El día 25 de diciembre fui a un concierto al aire libre de la Orquesta Sinfónica de Tenerife. ¡Fue guay!
El año que viene voy a pasar la Navidad con mi abuela, en Manchester.
Voy a decorar el árbol con mi abuela y mi hermana y también voy a comer un pudín de Navidad inglés. Va a ser genial.

3 Lee el texto otra vez. Termina las frases en inglés.

Ejemplo: **1** In Juanita's family, Christmas is a very important celebration.

1 In Juanita's family, Christmas is a very important …
2 In their house, they have a tree and …
3 On Christmas Eve they eat …
4 On Christmas Day they eat …
5 The Three Kings come on the …
6 Last year, Juanita went to …
7 On Christmas Day she listened to a …
8 Next year, Juanita is going to spend Christmas with her grandmother in …

4 Con tu compañero/a, habla de la Navidad.

¿Qué haces normalmente en Navidad?

¿Qué vas a hacer el año que viene?

¿Qué hiciste el año pasado?

Bebo cava.
Decoro el árbol de Navidad.
Voy a comer pudín.
Comí ternera asada.
Decoré el belén.
Voy a beber cava.
Bebí vino tinto.
Voy a decorar el árbol de Navidad.
Como pavo.

5 Escribe tus respuestas del ejercicio 4.

Checklist
● include three tenses
● use connectives such as porque, add at least two opinions
● make sure you have used the correct tenses
● pay careful attention to spelling, punctuation and accents

6 Comprueba las respuestas de tu compañero/a.

● Are any words misspelt?
● Are all accents in place?
● Has he/she used tenses correctly?
● Could he/she use some 'super Spanish', for example add more opinions, use more connectives?

Gramática

1 **Translate these questions into Spanish.**

Example: **1** ¿Cómo se llama tu instituto?

❶ What is your school called?
❷ How many pupils are there?
❸ How many lessons are there per day?
❹ How many teachers are there?
❺ Do you like your school?
❻ Do you wear uniform?

¿Cuántos …
¿Te …
¿Cómo …
¿Cuántas …
¿Llevas …
¿Cuántos …

2 **Choose the correct word. Write out the sentence and then translate it into English.**

Example: **1** ¿Te **gusta** el español?
Do you like Spanish?

❶ ¿Te **gusta** / **gustan** el español?
❷ No me **gusta** / **gustan** el español porque es **aburrido** / **aburrida**.
❸ ¿Te **gusta** / **gustan** las matemáticas?
❹ Me **gusta** / **gustan** mucho las matemáticas porque son **interesante** / **interesantes** y **divertidos** / **divertidas**.
❺ ¿Te **gusta** / **gustan** la música?

3 **Write out the near future-tense sentences correctly.**
Then translate them into English.

Example: **1** El año que viene voy a estudiar inglés.
Next year I am going to study English.

❶ Elañoquevienevoyaestudiaringlés
❷ Elañoquevienevoyaestudiarfrancés
❸ Elañoquevienevoyaestudiardiseño

❹ ¿Quévasaestudiarelañoqueviene?
❺ Elañoquevienevoyaestudiarteatro

4 **Read this conversation. Decide whether the sentences are in the present tense (P) or the near future tense (F).**

Example: **1** P

❶ – ¿Qué estudias?
❷ – Estudio inglés.
❸ – ¿Te gusta?
❹ – No, no me gusta nada: es un rollo.
❺ – ¿Qué vas a estudiar el año que viene?
❻ – El año que viene voy a estudiar español.
❼ – También voy a estudiar ciencias.
❽ – Me gustan las ciencias porque son interesantes

5 Complete the rules with the correct infinitives.

Example: **1** No se debe **llevar** zapatillas de deporte.

❶ No se debe _____ zapatillas de deporte.
❷ No se debe _____ chicle.
❸ No se debe _____ en los pasillos.
❹ No se debe _____ el móvil en clase.
❺ Se debe _____ en clase.
❻ Se debe _____ los deberes.
❼ Se debe _____ a tiempo.
❽ Se debe _____ uniforme.

hacer	comer
llegar	llevar
escuchar	correr
usar	llevar

 6 Put the verbs in brackets into the preterite tense.

Example: **1** llegué

Me gusta mucho el instituto. Es muy divertido.

Ayer **(1)**_____ *(llegar)* a las ocho de la mañana y **(2)**_____ *(ir)* a la clase de inglés. **(3)**_____ *(escuchar)* al profesor de inglés. La clase **(4)**_____ *(ser)* muy interesante.

En la hora de comer **(5)**_____ *(comer)* ensalada y **(6)**_____ *(beber)* agua. Luego **(7)**_____ *(cantar)* en el coro.

Más tarde, en la clase de español, **(8)**_____ *(estudiar)* mucho. **(9)**_____ *(escribir)* un poco y **(10)**_____ *(trabajar)* con el ordenador.

Después del colegio **(11)**_____ *(jugar)* al voleibol en el patio con mis amigos.

 7 Copy out the table and put the verbs in blue in the following text into the correct column.

Preterite	Present
	Me llamo

Me llamo Pablo y **voy** al instituto Cristóbal Colón en Barcelona. Ayer en el recreo **jugué** al baloncesto en el gimnasio. ¡**Fue** genial! Luego, después del colegio **toqué** la trompeta en la orquesta porque **me gusta** mucho la música. Un poco más tarde **hablé** con mis amigos en el patio.

Luego **fui** a la cafetería. **Comí** un bocadillo y **bebí** una limonada.

Después, en casa, estudié ciencias porque **tengo** un examen mañana. **Me gustan** mucho las ciencias pero mi profesor **es** un poco aburrido.

Palabras

Un día en el instituto

¿Cómo se llama tu instituto?

Mi instituto se llama …

¿Cuántos alumnos hay?

Hay … alumnos.

¿Cuántos profesores hay?

Hay … profesores.

¿Cuántas clases hay al día?

Hay … clases al día.

¿Llevas uniforme?

(No) llevo uniforme.

¿Te gusta tu instituto?

(No) me gusta mucho mi instituto.

En el recreo

¿Qué haces en el recreo?

Los lunes …

Los martes …

Los miércoles …

Los jueves …

Los viernes …

Voy …

al club de ajedrez

al club de informática

al club de teatro

al patio

a la cantina

Canto en el coro.

Juego al fútbol.

Toco en la orquesta.

Voy a la biblioteca.

A school day

What is your school called?

My school is called …

How many pupils are there?

There are … pupils.

How many teachers are there?

There are … teachers.

How many lessons are there in a day?

There are … lessons in a day.

Do you wear a uniform?

I (don't) wear a uniform.

Do you like your school?

I (don't) like my school very much.

In the break

What do you do at break?

On Mondays …

On Tuesdays …

On Wednesdays …

On Thursdays …

On Fridays …

I go …

to chess club

to computer club

to theatre club

to the playground

to the canteen

I sing in the choir.

I play football.

I play in the orchestra.

I go to the library.

Las asignaturas

el comercio

el dibujo

el diseño

el español

el francés

el inglés

el teatro

la educación física

la geografía

la historia

la informática

la música

la tecnología

las ciencias

las matemáticas

¿Qué estudias?

Estudio inglés.

¿Te gusta?

¿Por qué?

Porque es …

aburrido/a

creativo/a

divertido/a

importante

interesante

difícil

fácil

guay

útil

¿Qué vas a estudiar el año que viene?

El año que viene voy a estudiar …

¿Por qué te gusta(n)?

Me gusta(n) … porque es/son …

Subjects

business studies

art

design

Spanish

French

English

drama

PE

geography

history

ICT

music

technology

science(s)

maths

What do you study?

I study English.

Do you like it?

Why?

Because it's …

boring

creative

fun

important

interesting

difficult

easy

great

useful

What are you going to study next year?

Next year I'm going to study …

Why do you like it (them)?

I like … because it's/they're …

Las normas del instituto

Se debe …	*You must …*
escuchar en clase	*listen in class*
hacer los deberes	*do your homework*
llegar a tiempo	*arrive on time*
llevar uniforme	*wear uniform*
No se debe …	*You must not …*
comer chicle	*chew gum*
correr en los pasillos	*run in the corridors*
llevar joyas	*wear jewellery*
llevar maquillaje	*wear make-up*
llevar zapatillas de deporte	*wear trainers*
usar el móvil en clase	*use your mobile in class*

Timoteo el travieso — *Terrible Timothy*

Llegué a las once de la mañana.	*I arrived at 11 in the morning.*
No escuché al profesor.	*I didn't listen to the teacher.*
Escuché música.	*I listened to music.*
Salí en el recreo.	*I went out at break/lunch.*
Me compré un chicle.	*I bought some gum.*
Comí dos hamburguesas.	*I ate two hamburgers.*
Bebí una lata de Coca-Cola.	*I drank a can of Coke.*
Mandé mensajes a mis amigos.	*I sent texts to my friends.*
Saqué fotos con mi móvil.	*I took photos with my phone.*
Hablé por teléfono con mi hermano.	*I talked to my brother on the phone.*
No estudié mucho.	*I didn't study a lot.*
Jugué al fútbol en el patio.	*I played football in the playground.*
¿Te gusta el instituto?	*Do you like school?*
¿A qué hora llegaste ayer?	*What time did you arrive yesterday?*
¿Qué hiciste en el recreo?	*What did you do at break time?*
¿Qué hiciste en la clase de matemáticas?	*What did you do in maths?*

Palabras muy útiles — *Very useful words*

después	*after*
más tarde	*later*
normalmente	*normally*
todos los …	*every …*
ayer	*yesterday*
el año que viene	*next year*

Estrategia

Expressions with the infinitive

In Spanish there are many expressions which are always followed by an infinitive.

The ones you have seen in this module are these:

Voy a …	*I am going to …*
Se debe …	*You/One must …*
No se debe …	*You/One mustn't …*

Here are some others: can you remember what they mean?

Quiero …
Tengo que …
Me gusta …
Me gustaría …

Keep a list of these expressions on a special page of your vocab book. Write them with an infinitive to finish the sentence so that you have a full, correct example.

Here are some infinitives for you to choose from:
ir de vacaciones *(go on holiday)*
estudiar historia *(study history)*
hacer mis deberes *(do my homework)*
descargar música *(download music)*
llevar maquillaje *(wear make-up)*
chatear *(chat online)*

1 Me duele . . .

● Learning the parts of the body
● Using **me duele** and **me duelen**

1 Escucha y escribe la letra correcta. (1–15)

Ejemplo: **1** n

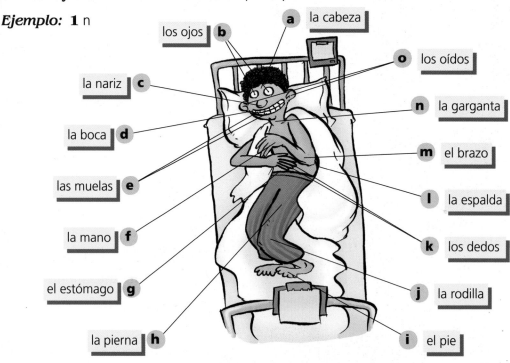

los ojos **b**

la cabeza **a**

los oídos **o**

la nariz **c**

la garganta **n**

la boca **d**

el brazo **m**

las muelas **e**

la espalda **l**

la mano **f**

los dedos **k**

el estómago **g**

la rodilla **j**

la pierna **h**

el pie **i**

2 Cierra el libro. Señala una parte de tu cuerpo. Tu compañero/a lo dice en español.

● (points to teeth)
■ las muelas

> Pay attention to these words. Listen and repeat each one carefully.
>
> *bra**z**o, nari**z**, cabe**z**a, **g**ar**g**anta, o**j**os, rodi**ll**a*

3 Escucha. Copia y rellena la tabla. (1–6)

	(a) Problem	(b) How long?
1	leg and foot	five days

You can't translate the word 'for' word for word into Spanish. In Spanish you say **desde hace**.

¿Qué te duele?
Me duele …, Me duelen …
¿Desde hace cuánto tiempo?
Desde hace   dos horas.
             tres días.
             una semana.

Gramática

doler *(to hurt)*

You need to use the definite article **el/la/los/las** after **doler**.

Singular
Me duel**e la** cabeza.   *My head hurts.*
Me duel**e el** pie.   *My foot hurts.*

Plural
Me duel**en las** piernas. *My feet hurt.*
Me duel**en los** ojos.   *My eyes hurt.*

¿Qué **te** duele?   *What hurts (you)?*

Para saber más   página 000

4 Escribe las frases correctamente.

Ejemplo: **1** Me duele el estómago desde hace dos horas.

 **1**  **2**   **3**  **4**  **5**  **6**

2 horas   **3 días**   **1 hora**   **1 semana**   **6 horas**   **4 horas**

 5 Con tu compañero/a, haz estos diálogos.

- ¿Qué te duele?
- Me duele <u>la pierna</u>.
- ¿Desde hace cuánto tiempo?
- Desde hace <u>cinco horas</u>.

1    **5 hours**

2   **3 days**

3    **2 hours**

4   **one week**

 6 Escucha y lee.

¿Qué te pasa, Margarita?
No me encuentro bien.
Me duelen las muelas
desde hace cuatro horas …

(Estribillo)

¿Qué te duele? ¿Qué te duele?
Tuve un accidente.
Ahora me duele el pie
y la cabeza también.

(Estribillo)

¿Qué te duele, Toño?
Me duele mucho la mano.
Me caí de mi caballo
¡Ay! ¡Ay! ¡Ay! ¡Qué tonto!

(Estribillo)

Me siento muy, muy mal.
Fatal … me siento fatal.
Me duele la garganta
desde hace una semana.

(Estribillo)

(Estribillo)
Tengo que ver al médico,
no me encuentro bien.
Tengo que ir al hospital,
me siento muy, muy mal.

no me encuentro bien = *I don't feel well*
me siento muy, muy mal = *I feel really bad*
tuve = *I had*
me caí de mi caballo = *I fell off my horse*
¡Qué tonto! = *How stupid!*

 7 Busca estas frases en español en la canción.

Ejemplo: **1** Tengo que ver al médico.

1 I have to see a doctor.
2 I have to go to hospital.
3 What's the matter, Miss?
4 My teeth hurt.

5 I had an accident.
6 Now my foot hurts!
7 My hand hurts a lot.
8 For a week.

2 En la farmacia

- Describing symptoms
- Using **estar** and **tener** to talk about ailments

 Escucha y escribe la letra correcta. (1–8)

Ejemplo: **1** c

Héctor Hipocondríaco

No me encuentro bien.

¿Qué te pasa?

a
Estoy enfermo.

b
Tengo fiebre.

c
Tengo diarrea.

d
Tengo tos.

e
Tengo gripe.

f
Tengo catarro.

g
Tengo vómitos.

h
Estoy cansado.

 Con tu compañero/a, haz diálogos.

- No me encuentro bien.
- ¿Qué te pasa?
- Tengo gripe.

Gramática

You use the verb **tener** *(to have)* to refer to most medical problems.

Tengo tos.	*I have a cough.*
Tienes tos.	*You have a cough.*
Tiene tos.	*He/She has a cough.*

But some expressions use the verb **estar** *(to be)*, followed by an adjective.

estoy	*I am*
estás	*you are*
está	*he/she/it is*

The adjective ending must agree with the subject:

Estoy cansado/a.   *I am tired.*

Para saber más   página 00

 Escucha y escribe las letras correctas. (1–6)

Ejemplo: **1** c

Tienes que …

a
tomar estas pastillas

b
tomar este jarabe

c
tomar estas aspirinas

d
beber agua

leer 4 Lee los textos. Escribe un remedio para cada persona.
(There may be more than one answer for each person.)

Ejemplo: **1** Tienes que tomar este jarabe.

1 Estoy enfermo. Estoy cansado y también tengo tos… **Javier**
2 Estoy enferma.Tengo diarrea y también tengo vómitos. ¿Qué me pasa? **Belén**
3 No me encuentro bien. Tengo fiebre. También estoy cansado. Creo que tengo gripe… **Antonio**
4 Me duele mucho la garganta y estoy cansada todo el tiempo… **María**
5 Tengo catarro. Me duele la cabeza y la garganta. No me encuentro bien… **Patricia**

 escuchar 5 Escucha y escribe la letra del dibujo que <u>no</u> se menciona. (1–6)

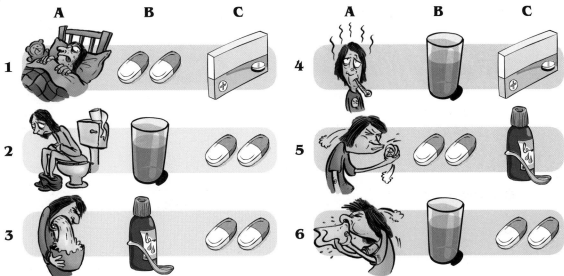

 hablar 6 Con tu compañero/a, haz estos diálogos.

● Estoy <u>enfermo/a</u>.
■ ¿Qué te pasa?
● <u>Tengo fiebre</u>.
■ Tienes que <u>beber agua</u> y también tienes que <u>tomar estas aspirinas</u>.
● Gracias.

> You can join sentences together using phrases like **y también** *(and also)*. Make sure you check you have the right ending on enferm**o**/enferm**a**.

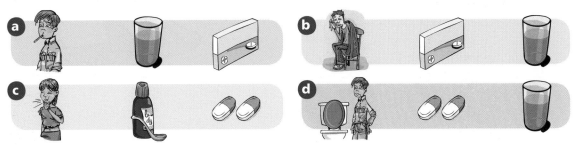

 escribir 7 Escribe tres diálogos. Utiliza los dibujos del ejercicio 6.

- Talking about healthy and unhealthy food
- Using adverbs of frequency

 1 Pon la comida en la columna correcta.

	Comida sana	Comida malsana
	verduras	

verduras **galletas** **patatas fritas** **Coca-Cola**

fruta **pescado** **café** **caramelos**

huevos **leche** **agua** **pasteles**

 2 Escucha y comprueba tus respuestas.

 3 Escucha y apunta las respuestas de Angelina. (1–6)

Ejemplo: **1** fish b

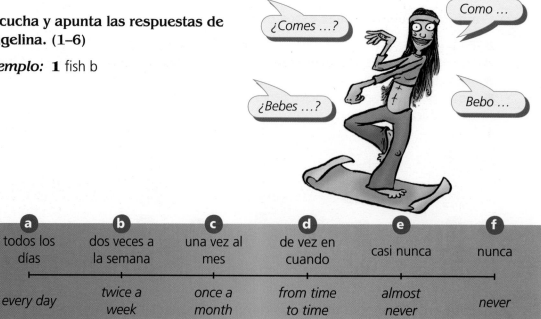

¿Comes …?
Como …
¿Bebes …?
Bebo …

a	b	c	d	e	f
todos los días	dos veces a la semana	una vez al mes	de vez en cuando	casi nunca	nunca
every day	twice a week	once a month	from time to time	almost never	never

4 Lee los textos. ¿Quién habla? (1–3)

Alicia   *Pepe*   *Javier*   *Bárbara*

1 Pues…, como pasteles y caramelos todos los días. Me gustan mucho, pero son malsanos. De vez en cuando como comida sana, por ejemplo pescado o huevos. Nunca como patatas fritas. No me gustan nada.

2 Como fruta de vez en cuando pero nunca como verduras. No me gustan nada las verduras ¡Buagh! Bebo agua todos los días, pero casi nunca bebo leche. ¡La leche es para los bebés!

3 Bebo agua todos los días, pero también bebo Coca-Cola dos veces a la semana. Nunca bebo café. No me gusta nada. Como pescado una vez al mes: me gusta bastante. Pero nunca como fruta. No me gusta.

 5 Con tu compañero/a, pregunta y contesta.

- ● ¿Comes <u>patatas fritas</u>?
- ■ A ver… <u>No. Nunca</u> como <u>patatas fritas</u>.
- ● ¿Bebes <u>agua</u>?
- ■ <u>Sí</u>, bebo <u>agua todos los días</u>.

> Use these phrases to add expression and make your Spanish sound more authentic:
>
> A ver…   *Well…*
> ¡Buagh!   *Yuck!*
> ¡Claro que sí!   *Of course*
> No mucho   *Not a lot*

 never   **every day**   **twice a week**    **once a month**

 from time to time    **hardly ever**    **never**

 6 Escribe un párrafo.

Todos los días	
Dos veces a la semana	
Una vez al mes	como …
De vez en cuando	bebo …
Casi nunca	
Nunca	

Me gusta mucho.
Me gusta**n** mucho.
No me gusta nada.
No me gusta**n** nada.

Mini-test

I can
- ● name parts of the body
- ● say what hurts
- ● describe my symptoms and get a remedy
- ● name healthy and unhealthy food
- **G** use the verbs **tener** and **estar**
- **G** use adverbs of frequency

- Talking about healthy living
- Using the near future with **ir a** … + infinitive

1 Escucha y escribe la letra correcta. (1–6)

¿Qué vas a hacer para llevar una vida más sana?

Para llevar una vida más sana …

Ejemplo: **1** b

Voy a …

a hacer deporte

b dormir ocho horas al día

c beber agua

d comer fruta y verduras

No voy a …

e comer comida basura

f fumar cigarrillos

g tomar drogas

h beber alcohol

Llevar is a verb that means different things in English. It can mean *to lead* (life), *to carry* (objects) or *to wear* (clothes).

para = *in order to*
llevar una vida más sana = *lead a more healthy life*

2 Con tu compañero/a, haz estos diálogos.

- ¿Qué vas a hacer para llevar una vida más sana?
- Para llevar una vida más sana <u>voy a hacer deporte</u>. También <u>voy a dormir ocho horas al día</u>. Y <u>no voy a comer comida basura</u>.

Voy a …	También voy a …	No voy a …
1		
2		
3		
4		

Gramática

The near future

ir *(to go)* + **a** + infinitive

(I)	voy		hacer
(you)	vas		dormir
(he/she/it)	va	a	beber
(we)	vamos		tomar
(you pl.)	vais		comer
(they)	van		fumar

Voy a beber agua.
    I am going to drink water.
¿Vas a hacer deporte?
    Are you going to do sport?

Para saber más   página 00

leer 3 Copia las frases con el infinitivo correcto.

Ejemplo: **1** Voy a hacer deporte.

1 Voy a **fumar** / **hacer** / **beber** deporte.
2 No voy a **comer** / **tomar** / **fumar** cigarrillos.
3 Voy a **comer** / **hacer** / **beber** agua.
4 Voy a **comer** / **fumar** / **dormir** fruta y verduras.
5 No voy a **tener** / **tomar** / **salir** drogas.
6 No voy a **escuchar** / **beber** / **hablar** alcohol.
7 Voy a **dormir** / **hacer** / **comer** ocho horas al día.
8 No voy a **jugar** / **comer** / **leer** comida basura.

leer 4 Lee los textos. ¿Verdadero (V) o falso (F)?

Ejemplo: **1** V

tampoco = *neither*

Voy a comer fruta y verduras y voy a beber agua. También voy a hacer deporte y voy a dormir ocho horas al día. No voy a comer comida basura. No me gustan nada las hamburguesas. No voy a fumar cigarrillos. No voy a tomar drogas. Y no voy a beber alcohol. Voy a llevar una vida sana.
Susana Sana

A ver… no voy a comer fruta ni verduras ¡buagh! No voy a beber agua: no me gusta nada. Prefiero beber alcohol. No voy a hacer deporte. ¡Qué aburrido! Voy a comer comida basura. Me encantan las hamburguesas, ¡qué ricas! No voy a fumar cigarrillos pero no voy a llevar una vida sana. No gracias.
Miguel Malsano

1 Susana va a comer fruta y verduras y va a beber agua.
2 Susana va a comer comida basura.
3 Susana no va a fumar cigarrillos.
4 Susana va a beber alcohol.

5 Miguel no va a beber agua.
6 Miguel va a hacer deporte.
7 Miguel va a comer comida basura.
8 Miguel va a fumar cigarrillos.

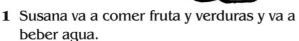

escribir 5 Escribe un párrafo sobre tu vida.

● Say what you eat every day	Todos los días …
● Say what you sometimes eat	A veces, como …
● Say what you never eat	Nunca como …
● Add in details about what you like/don't like	(No) Me gusta comer …
● Talk about what you will eat in the future	En el futuro voy a comer …
● Talk about what you won't eat	Pero no voy a comer …
● Say what you are going to do to lead a more healthy life	Para llevar una vida más sana, voy a …
	También voy a …
	Pero no voy a …

5 Mañana, mañana . . .

● Making resolutions
● Using two tenses together

escuchar **1** Escucha y lee. Escribe un nombre para cada letra.

a **b** **c** **d**

> Estoy enfermo. Me duele el estómago.
> Tengo vómitos y diarrea.
> ¡Qué horror! Voy a tomar estas
> pastillas y mañana voy a cambiar mi
> vida. En el futuro, voy a dormir ocho
> horas al día y voy a beber mucha agua.
>
> **Antonio**

> Me duele la cabeza, la garganta… También
> tengo tos. No me encuentro bien. Voy a tomar
> unas pastillas y este jarabe. Mañana voy a
> cambiar. Voy a llevar una vida más sana. No voy
> a fumar nunca más. La semana que viene voy a
> hacer deporte todos los días y en el futuro voy a
> llevar una dieta mucho más sana.
>
> **Jessica**

> Yo tengo fiebre. Me duelen las manos y los
> pies. No me encuentro bien. Voy a tomar estas
> aspirinas. Mañana voy a cambiar mi vida. Voy a
> llevar una dieta más sana. La semana que viene,
> voy a comer fruta y verduras. Normalmente como
> comida malsana. Voy a cambiar todo y voy a ser
> una persona nueva.
>
> **Juan**

> Yo me encuentro bien. Como bien por
> lo general. Nunca como pasteles ni
> caramelos. Tampoco bebo alcohol y nunca
> fumo. Ahora voy a beber un té – sin leche
> – y luego voy a leer mi libro preferido y
> escuchar música clásica. Voy a comer fruta
> y verduras y voy a beber mucha agua.
>
> **Carolina**

sin = *without*
voy a cambiar mi vida = *I am going to change my life*

leer **2** Corrige los errores en estas frases.

Ejemplo: **1** Antonio tiene vómitos y diarrea.

1 Antonio tiene fiebre y diarrea.
2 Antonio va a tomar unas aspirinas.
3 Jessica tiene catarro.
4 Va a fumar un paquete de cigarrillos.
5 Juan tiene tos.
6 La semana que viene va a comer comida basura.
7 Carolina come muchos pasteles.
8 Carolina no va a beber mucha agua.

> The housemates use these phrases
> to talk about resolutions for the
> future:
>
> mañana = *tomorrow*
> la semana que viene = *next week*
> en el futuro = *in the future*

Escucha. ¿Quién habla? ¿Usa presente (P) o futuro (F)? (1–4)
Who's speaking? Are they using the present (P) or the near future tense (F)? (1–4)

Ejemplo: **1** Antonio P

 Con tu compañero/a, haz estos diálogos.

- ● ¿Qué te pasa?
- ■ Me duele la cabeza y me duele la garganta también.
- ● ¿Qué vas a hacer?
- ■ Voy a beber agua y no voy a beber alcohol.

 Escribe un párrafo para Pepe o Rosa.

Estoy enfermo/enferma.
Tengo …
Me duele …
Me duelen …
Voy a …
En el futuro, voy a …
No voy a …

Pepe

Rosa

- • tomar aspirinas
- • beber mucha agua

En el futuro

- • cambiar
- • llevar una dieta más sana
- • hacer deporte

- • tomar drogas
- • beber alcohol

- • tomar pastillas
- • beber mucha agua

En el futuro

- • dormir ocho horas al día
- • beber agua
- • comer fruta y verduras

- • comer comida basura
- • fumar cigarrillos

Resumen

Unidad 1

I can

- name the parts of the body — la cabeza, el brazo, las piernas, los pies
- ask someone what hurts — ¿Qué te duele?
- ask how long something has been a problem — ¿Desde hace cuánto tiempo?
- say how long something has been a problem — Desde hace tres días.
- **G** use **me duele** and **me duelen** — Me duel**e** la espalda. Me duel**en** los ojos.

Unidad 2

I can

- describe different symptoms — Estoy enfermo. Tengo fiebre.
- ask someone what the matter is — ¿Qué te pasa?
- suggest a remedy — Tienes que tomar este jarabe. Tienes que beber agua.
- **G** use **tener** and **estar** to talk about health — **Estoy** cansado. **Tengo** gripe. **Tengo** catarro.

Unidad 3

I can

- name healthy and unhealthy foods — pescado, leche, agua, caramelos, pasteles, patatas fritas
- ask what someone eats or drinks — ¿Comes verduras? ¿Bebes Coca-Cola?
- use frequency expressions — **Nunca** como verduras. Como verduras **de vez en cuando**.

Unidad 4

I can

- say what I am going to do to lead a healthy life — Para llevar una vida más sana voy a dormir ocho horas al día.
- ask someone what they will do — ¿Qué vas a hacer para llevar una vida más sana?
- **G** use the near future tense — Voy a hacer deporte. Va a beber agua.

Unidad 5

I can

- make resolutions — Voy a cambiar. Voy a tener una dieta más sana.
- use time expressions to talk about the future — mañana, en el futuro, la semana que viene
- **G** use two tenses together — Me duele la cabeza y tengo fiebre. Mañana voy a cambiar mi vida … No voy a beber alcohol …

Prepárate

 3

 1 Escucha. Copia y rellena la tabla. (1–5)

	Problem	Remedy
1	sore back	take pills

 **2** Con tu compañero/a, pregunta y contesta.

● ¿Qué vas a hacer para llevar una vida más sana?

■ Voy a …/No voy a …

a    **b**   **c**    **d**

e   **f**    **g**   **h**

 3 Lee el texto y termina las frases en inglés.

Ejemplo: **1** Alicia likes sport.

> Me gusta mucho hacer deporte. Juego al fútbol todos los sábados y hago natación dos veces a la semana. Pero también me gusta comer hamburguesas. Nunca bebo alcohol y casi nunca bebo café.
>
> Para llevar una vida más sana voy a comer más fruta y verduras y no voy a comer hamburguesas pero … ¡me gustan tanto!
>
> Alicia

tanto = *so much*

1 Alicia likes …   **4** But she also likes …

2 Every Saturday …   **5** She never …

3 Twice a week …   **6** To be more healthy …

 4 Escribe un párrafo utilizando estas notas.

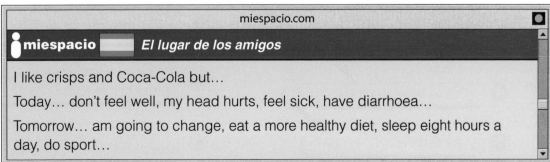

miespacio.com

miespacio   *El lugar de los amigos*

I like crisps and Coca-Cola but…

Today… don't feel well, my head hurts, feel sick, have diarrhoea…

Tomorrow… am going to change, eat a more healthy diet, sleep eight hours a day, do sport…

Escucha. Copia el texto y rellena los espacios en blanco con palabras del dibujo.

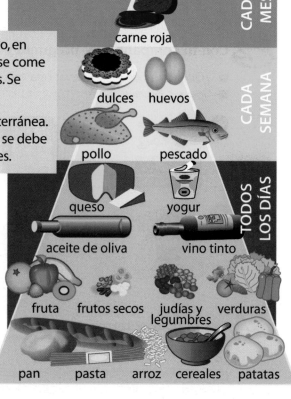

	CADA MES
carne roja	
dulces huevos	CADA SEMANA
pollo pescado	
queso yogur	TODOS LOS DÍAS
aceite de oliva vino tinto	
fruta frutos secos judías y legumbres verduras	
pan pasta arroz cereales patatas	

La dieta mediterránea es una dieta muy sana. Por ejemplo, en España, se come mucha **(1)** *fruta y verduras*. También se come **(2)** ~~~, pasta, **(3)** ~~~, cereales o patatas todos los días. Se puede beber **(4)** ~~~ con moderación.

El **(5)** ~~~ también es muy importante en la dieta mediterránea. Se come cada semana **(6)** ~~~, pollo y **(7)** ~~~. Pero no se debe comer mucha **(8)** ~~~: se puede comer alguna vez al mes.

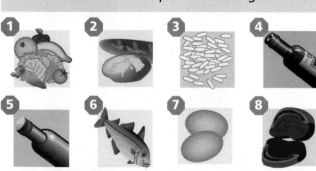

se come = *is/are eaten*
se puede comer = *you can eat*
cada semana = *each week*
alguna vez al mes = *a few times per month*

2 **Empareja las preguntas con las respuestas correctas.**

Ejemplo: **1** c

En la dieta mediterránea …

1 ¿Qué se come todos los días?

2 ¿Qué se puede beber con moderación?

3 ¿Qué es muy importante?

4 ¿Qué no se debe comer mucho?

5 ¿Qué se come cada semana?

a Vino tinto.

b Pescado, pollo y huevos.

c Pan, pasta, arroz, cereales o patatas.

d En la dieta mediterránea el aceite de oliva es muy importante.

e En la dieta mediterránea no se debe comer mucha carne roja.

3 Con tu compañero/a, pregunta y contesta.

● ¿Qué se puede comer todos los días?

● ¿Qué se puede comer cada semana?

● ¿Qué se puede comer alguna vez al mes?

Like **(no) se debe, (no) se puede** is an impersonal verb. It means *you can (not)*.

se debe = *you must*
no se debe = *you must not*
se puede = *you can*
no se puede = *you cannot*

Se puede comer patatas todos los días.
You can eat potatoes every day.
No se puede comer mucha carne.
You can't eat much meat.
¿Qué se puede beber con moderación?
What can you drink in moderation?

leer 4 Lee el texto. Empareja las preguntas con las respuestas apropiadas.

Ejemplo: **1** b

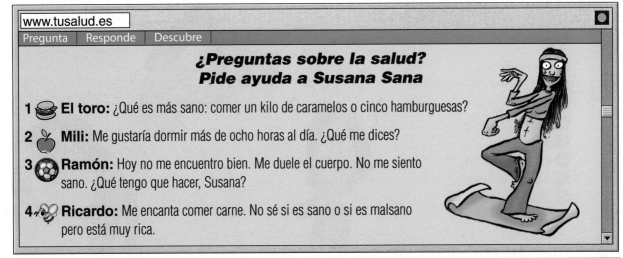

www.tusalud.es

Pregunta | Responde | Descubre

¿Preguntas sobre la salud?
Pide ayuda a Susana Sana

1 El toro: ¿Qué es más sano: comer un kilo de caramelos o cinco hamburguesas?

2 Mili: Me gustaría dormir más de ocho horas al día. ¿Qué me dices?

3 Ramón: Hoy no me encuentro bien. Me duele el cuerpo. No me siento sano. ¿Qué tengo que hacer, Susana?

4 Ricardo: Me encanta comer carne. No sé si es sano o si es malsano pero está muy rica.

www.tusalud.es

a Comer mucha carne puede ser malo para la salud. Para comer bien, también hay que comer fruta y verduras.

b ¡Qué horror! ¡Comes hamburguesas¡ ¡Y también caramelos! Necesitas una dieta equilibrada. Prueba la dieta mediterránea.

c Tienes que salir y hacer deporte. ¡Muévete! Por favor, respétate.

d La regla de 'los tres ochos': ocho horas para dormir, ocho para trabajar y ocho con tu familia es una regla muy sana. Si duermes más, vas a tener problemas de insomnio.

 5 Lee los textos del ejercicio 4 otra vez. Busca estas frases en español.

Ejemplo: **1** ¿Qué es más sano?

1 What is more healthy?

2 I would like to sleep

3 I don't feel well today

4 I love to eat meat.

5 In order to eat well

6 you need a balanced diet

7 you have to get out and do sport

8 you are going to have problems with insomnia

Gramática

1 *Choose the correct part of* **doler** *and fill in the gaps with* **el/la/los** *or* **las.**

Example: **1** Me <u>duele la</u> mano desde hace dos horas.

1 Me **duele** / **duelen** ~~~ mano desde hace dos horas.
2 Me **duele** / **duelen** ~~~ piernas desde hace tres días.
3 ¿Te **duele** / **duelen** ~~~ ojos?
4 ¿Desde hace cuánto tiempo te **duele** / **duelen** ~~~ garganta?
5 ¿Qué te **duele** / **duelen**?
6 No me **duele** / **duelen** mucho ~~~ pies.
7 Me **duele** / **duelen** ~~~ estómago.
8 Me **duele** / **duelen** ~~~ brazo y me **duele** / **duelen** ~~~ pierna.

2 *Translate the following sentences into English.*

Example: **1** He/She has a temperature.

1 Tiene fiebre.
2 Estamos enfermos.
3 Tienen catarro.
4 Están cansadas.
5 Tienes tos.
6 Estás enfermo.
7 Tengo vómitos.
8 Estoy cansado.

3 *Copy out the conversation and fill in the gaps with the correct part of* **tener** *or* **estar.**

Isabel:	No me encuentro bien. **(1)** Estoy enferma. Me duele la cabeza y **(2)** _____ vómitos.
Felipe:	Yo no **(3)** _____ vómitos pero tampoco me siento bien. **(4)** _____ fiebre y **(5)** _____ muy cansado.
Isabel:	¿**(6)** _____ cansado? A ver… ¿**(7)** _____ tos también?
Felipe:	No, mi hermano **(8)** _____ tos pero yo no. Yo **(9)** _____ fiebre.
Isabel:	Mamá, Felipe **(10)** _____ fiebre y **(11)** _____ cansado pero no **(12)** _____ tos, ¿qué le pasa?
Mamá de Isabel:	Pues… **(13)** _____ enfermo…
Isabel y Felipe:	**(14)** _____ enfermos, muy enfermos…

tengo (×4)   estoy (×2)   tiene (×3)   tienes   estás   está (×2)   estamos

4 Put these sentences into order of frequency. 1 = most often, 6 = never.

Example: **1** Bebo agua todos los días.

De vez en cuando como patatas fritas.

Casi nunca como caramelos.

Dos veces a la semana como huevos.

Nunca como pescado.

Bebo agua todos los días.

Como pasteles una vez al mes.

 5 Find the eight infinitive forms in this balloon.
Write out their English meaning.

ir	hago	dormir	juegas	hacer
	comen	tomar	voy	comer
	fumamos	beber	fumar	jugar

 6 Complete the sentences with the correct infinitive, then translate them into English.

Example: **1** Voy a **dormir** ocho horas al día. *I am going to sleep 8 hours per day.*

1 Voy a _____ ocho horas al día.
2 Vamos a _____ deporte.
3 No va a _____ alcohol.
4 Voy a _____ fruta y verduras.
5 No van a _____ cigarrillos.
6 Vas a _____ agua.
7 Vais a _____ drogas.
8 No voy a _____ comida basura.

 7 Copy out the text with the correct verbs.

Example: Normalmente como …

Normalmente **como / voy a comer** patatas fritas y muchos pasteles y no **hago / voy a hacer** mucho deporte, pero esta semana **como / voy a comer** bien y **hago / voy a hacer** mucho deporte. Eso es muy importante para llevar una vida sana. El lunes **hago / voy a hacer** natación, el martes **juego / voy a jugar** al voleibol y el jueves **juego / voy a jugar** al fútbol.

Palabras

El cuerpo	The body
el brazo	arm
el estómago	stomach
el pie	foot
la boca	mouth
la cabeza	head
la espalda	back
la garganta	throat
la mano	hand
la nariz	nose
la pierna	leg
la rodilla	knee
los dedos	fingers
las muelas	teeth
los oídos	ears
los ojos	eyes
¿Qué te duele?	What hurts?
Me duele la pierna.	My leg hurts.
Me duelen las muelas.	My teeth hurt.
¿Desde hace cuánto tiempo?	For how long?
Desde hace …	For …
dos horas	two hours
tres días	three days
una semana	a week

¿Qué te pasa?	What's the matter?
No me encuentro bien.	I don't feel well.
Estoy cansado/a.	I'm tired.
Estoy enfermo/a.	I'm ill.
Tengo catarro.	I've got a cold.
Tengo diarrea.	I've got diarrhoea.
Tengo fiebre.	I've got a temperature.
Tengo gripe.	I've got flu.
Tengo tos.	I've got a cough.
Tengo vómitos.	I've been sick.

Tienes que …	You have to …
beber agua	drink water
tomar estas aspirinas	take these aspirins
tomar estas pastillas	take these tablets
tomar este jarabe	take this syrup

Una dieta sana	A healthy diet
la comida sana	healthy food
la comida malsana	unhealthy food
el agua (f)	water
el café	coffee
el pescado	fish
la Coca-Cola	Coca-cola
la fruta	fruit
la leche	milk
las galletas	biscuits
las patatas fritas	crisps
las verduras	vegetables
los caramelos	sweets
los huevos	eggs
los pasteles	cakes
Bebo café todos los días.	I drink coffee every day.
Como caramelos dos veces a la semana.	I eat sweets twice a week.
Como fruta de vez en cuando.	I eat fruit from time to time.
Como patatas fritas una vez al mes.	I eat crisps once a month.
Casi nunca bebo leche.	I hardly ever drink milk.
Nunca como huevos.	I never eat eggs.
¡Buagh!	Yuck!
A ver…	Let's see…
¡Claro que sí!	Of course!
No mucho.	Not a lot.

La vida sana — *Healthy life*

Para llevar una vida más sana … — *To lead a healthier life …*

Voy a … — *I'm going to …*
- beber agua — *drink water*
- comer fruta y verduras — *eat fruit and vegetables*
- dormir ocho horas al día — *sleep eight hours a night*
- hacer deporte — *do sport*

No voy a … — *I'm not going to …*
- beber alcohol — *drink alcohol*
- comer comida basura — *eat junk food*
- fumar cigarrillos — *smoke cigarettes*
- tomar drogas — *take drugs*

Palabras muy útiles — *Very useful words*

desde hace — *for (length of time)*
nunca — *never*
de vez en cuando — *from time to time*
también — *also*
para — *in order to*
ayer — *yesterday*
normalmente — *normally*
mañana — *tomorrow*
tampoco — *(n)either*

Estrategia

Learning new vocabulary

- Make your own word games. For example, write down the Spanish words you need to learn in one column and their English translations in another. Cut them up and play a game of pairs. Say each Spanish word to yourself as you pick it up.

la mano	hand
la pierna	leg
el pie	foot

- Next, take your learning further. In your vocabulary lists, highlight the words you definitely know in green. Highlight the ones you don't know in pink. Work harder at learning the pink words. When you think you know a pink word, draw a star by it.

Ganarse la vida

 4

1 Mi dinero

- Talking about earning and spending money
- Using **hacer** (to do) and **poner** (to put)

escuchar 1 Escucha y escribe las letras correctas. (1–9)

¿Qué haces para ganar dinero?

Ejemplo: **1** c

a  Lavo el coche.

b  Hago de canguro.

c Limpio la casa.

d Paseo al perro.

e Paso la aspiradora.

f Pongo la mesa.

g Plancho la ropa.

h Reparto periódicos.

i No hago nada.

Gramática

hacer *(to do/make)*		**poner** *(to put/lay)*	
hago	*I do/make*	**pongo**	*I put/lay*
haces	*you do/make*	pones	*you put/lay*
hace	*he/she/it does/makes*	pone	*he/she/it puts/lays*

Para saber más   página XXX

escuchar 2 Empareja las fotos con las frases correctas.
Luego escucha y comprueba tus respuestas. (1–8)

¿Qué haces con tu dinero?

Ejemplo: **1** f

1
2
3
4
5
6
7
8

- **a** Compro maquillaje.
- **b** Compro CDs o DVDs.
- **c** Compro ropa.
- **d** Compro videojuegos.
- **e** Compro crédito para mi móvil.
- **f** Compro revistas.
- **g** Compro chocolate y caramelos.
- **h** Ahorro.

escribir 3 *Write out the text in this word snake correctly.*

ParaganardinerolavoelcocheyaveceslimpiolacasaTambiénpaseoalperroyhagode
cangurolosfinesdesemanaConmidinerocomprocréditoparamimóvilyahorro.

4 **Escucha. Copia y rellena la tabla. (1–5)**

		Which chore?	He/She buys ...
1	Javier	delivers papers	magazines
2	Marta		
3	Fernanda		
4	Carolina		
5	Tomás		

 5 **Escucha otra vez. ¿Con qué frecuencia? ¿Y ahorra? (1–5)**

		Frecuencia	¿Ahorra? ✓/✗
1	Javier	todos los días	✗

> Listen for the following expressions and try to use them in your speaking too.
>
> | todos los días | every day |
> | a veces | sometimes |
> | los fines de semana | at the weekend |

6 **Con tu compañero/a, pregunta y contesta.**

- ● ¿Qué haces para ganar dinero?
- ■ Lavo el coche y también hago de canguro.
- ● ¿Qué haces con tu dinero?
- ■ Compro revistas y a veces compro CDs o DVDs.
- ● ¿Ahorras también?
- ■ No, no ahorro./Sí, ahorro. Quiero comprar …

 7 **Escucha la canción y rellena los espacios en blanco con las palabras del cuadro.**

| ropa | videojuegos | caramelos |
| revistas | perro | crédito |

Yo no quiero ahorrar,
tengo poco dinero
porque me encanta gastar.

Gano mucho dinero todos los días
y luego, cuando puedo, compro **(1)** _____.
Hago de canguro, lavo y plancho la **(2)** _____
Voy a la cafetería donde tomo una sopa.
Luego voy al centro comercial
y compro **(3)** _____ para mi móvil.

Yo no quiero ahorrar,
tengo poco dinero
porque me encanta gastar.

Paseo al **(4)** _____ y reparto periódicos,
luego compro caramelos y **(5)** _____.
Trabajo mucho, pongo la mesa,
compro CDs, DVDs y a veces **(6)** _____.
Nunca compro maquillaje,
prefiero de vez en cuando ir de viaje …

Yo no quiero ahorrar,
tengo poco dinero
porque me encanta gastar.

gastar = *to spend*

Escucha y lee. (1–9)

¿Qué tipo de persona eres?

 **1** Soy activo.
Soy activa.

 2 Soy creativo.
Soy creativa.

 3 Soy práctico.
Soy práctica.

 4 Soy organizado.
Soy organizada.

 **5** Soy hablador.
Soy habladora.

 6 Soy fuerte.

 **7** Soy paciente.

 **8** Soy independiente.

 **9** Soy inteligente.

Gramática

Adjectival endings

Masculino	Femenino
activo	activa
hablador	habladora
inteligente	inteligente

In the feminine:
- **-o** changes to **-a**
- add **-a** to words ending in **-or**
- **-e** stays the same

Para saber más   página 000

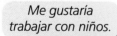 **2** **Con tu compañero/a, pregunta y contesta.**

- ¿Qué tipo de persona eres?
- Soy activo y también soy práctico.
  Soy activa y también soy práctica.

1 active + practical	**4** strong + patient
2 talkative + creative	**5** intelligent + independent
3 organized + independent	

3 **¿Quién habla? Escucha y escribe el nombre correcto. (1–9)**

Ejemplo: **1** Víctor

¿Qué te gustaría hacer?

 Me gustaría trabajar con niños.

Lía

Me gustaría trabajar con animales.

Ana

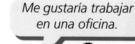 Me gustaría trabajar en una oficina.

Álvaro

 Me gustaría trabajar al aire libre.

María

 Me gustaría trabajar solo.

José

Me gustaría trabajar con gente.

Víctor

 Me gustaría hacer un trabajo manual.

Ramón

 Me gustaría hacer un trabajo creativo.

Belén

 Me gustaría viajar.

Diego

Gramática

Me gustaría is the conditional form of **me gusta**. Use it with the infinitive to say you *would* (or *wouldn't*) *like* to do something:

Me gustaría trabajar.	*I would like to work.*
Me gustaría viajar.	*I would like to travel.*
No me gustaría trabajar con niños.	*I wouldn't like to work with children.*

Para saber más — página 00

4 Con tu compañero/a, pregunta y contesta.

1 ¿Te gustaría trabajar con niños o con animales?
2 ¿Te gustaría trabajar en una oficina o al aire libre?
3 ¿Te gustaría trabajar solo/sola o con gente?
4 ¿Te gustaría viajar?
5 ¿Te gustaría hacer un trabajo creativo o un trabajo manual?
6 ¿Qué te gustaría hacer?

o = or

Where there are two vowels together, make sure you pronounce both sounds. In English they sometimes merge into one sound, e.g. 'air'. Listen and practise saying these words:

*ai*re *via*jar
*crea*tivo man*ual*

5 Lee el texto y contesta a las preguntas en inglés.

1 What sort of a person is Paco?
2 What type of work would he like to do?

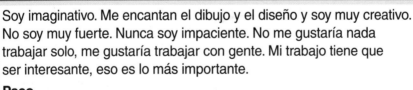

Soy imaginativo. Me encantan el dibujo y el diseño y soy muy creativo. No soy muy fuerte. Nunca soy impaciente. No me gustaría nada trabajar solo, me gustaría trabajar con gente. Mi trabajo tiene que ser interesante, eso es lo más importante.

Paco

6 Describe lo que te gustaría hacer.

Soy .../No soy ...
Nunca soy ...
Me gustaría ...
No me gustaría ...
Mi trabajo tiene que ser ...
  interesante/creativo/práctico ...

After you've finished, check your text carefully:
● Have you used the correct endings with the adjectives?
● Have you used infinitives correctly after **me gustaría**?
● Have you used accents correctly on words like **práctico** and **gustaría**?

1 Escucha y lee. Escribe tres datos sobre Henry en inglés.

Ejemplo: Henry is 25.

Me llamo Henry. Tengo veinticinco años. Soy inglés. Trabajo en un hotel en España.

Los idiomas son muy importantes en mi trabajo. Hablo inglés, por supuesto. Hablo bien español y francés, y también un poco de alemán. Me encantan los idiomas.

Trabajo principalmente con gente. No me gustaría trabajar solo.

Hablo inglés con clientes de Inglaterra, Francia o Alemania. Normalmente no hablan español.

También hablo en español con los camareros, la recepcionista, el cocinero y el servicio de limpieza.

Hago reservas para los clientes y soluciono problemas.

Hablo mucho por teléfono y también mando correos en inglés, francés, español y alemán.

A veces voy de excursión en autobús con mis clientes pero normalmente estoy en el hotel.

por supuesto = *of course*	el cocinero = *chef*
alemán = *German*	la recepcionista = *receptionist*
idiomas = *languages*	el servicio de limpieza = *cleaning staff*
los camareros = *waiters*	

2 Busca el equivalente en español en el texto.

Ejemplo: **1** soy

1 I am
2 I work
3 I speak
4 I would not like

5 I make reservations
6 I solve problems
7 I send emails

3 *Why are languages important in Henry's work? Make a list in English. He gives seven reasons.*

4 Eres Henry. Con tu compañero/a, pregunta y contesta.

- ¿Cuántos años tienes?
- Tengo …
- ¿Dónde trabajas?
- Trabajo en …
- ¿Qué idiomas hablas?
- Hablo … y …
- ¿Qué haces en tu trabajo?
- Hago …/Hablo …/Mando …/Voy …

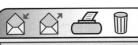 **5** Copia y completa el texto con los verbos del cuadro.

Ejemplo: **1** voy a estudiar

El año que viene **(1)** mandarín. Los idiomas son muy importantes en

mi trabajo. En el futuro **(2)** por todo el mundo. **(3)** ser

director de un hotel en China. **(4)** otros países y **(5)** en hoteles.

Conocer a culturas diferentes es una experiencia muy, muy buena.

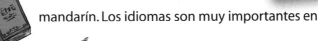
me gustaría   voy a trabajar   voy a visitar   voy a estudiar   voy a viajar

 6 Escucha y contesta en inglés a las preguntas sobre cada persona. (1–3)

1 What does he/she do in their current job?
2 What is he/she going to do next year?

 7 Eres Henry. Prepara una presentación.

Now (present tense)
I work in an office	Trabajo …
I talk to people	Hablo …
I solve problems	Soluciono …
I send emails	Mando …
I talk on the phone	Hablo …

Future (near future tense)
El año que viene
Going to:
study French	Voy a estudiar
work in a hotel	Voy a trabajar
travel	Voy a viajar

Mini-test

I can …
- talk about earning and spending money
- say what I'm like
- say what sort of work I'd like to do
- talk about using languages at work
- G use adjectival endings
- G use **me gustaría**

1 Escucha y escribe la letra correcta. (1–10)

Ejemplo: **1** d

¿En qué trabajas?

Soy …

 **a** diseñador/diseñador**a**

 **b** cociner**o**/cociner**a**

 **c** profesor/profesor**a**

 **d** camarer**o**/camarer**a**

 **e** enfermer**o**/enfermer**a**

 **f** ingenier**o**/ingenier**a**

 **g** médic**o**/médic**a**

 **h** futbolista

i recepcionista

j policía

In Spanish, leave out the indefinite article (**un** or **una**) when talking about your job.

Soy profesor.   *I am a teacher.*
¿Eres recepcionista?   *Are you a receptionist?*

The words for many jobs end in **-o** in the masculine and **-a** in the feminine.
Some jobs are the same in both.

2 Escucha y escribe el trabajo correcto. (1–10)

Ejemplo: **1** profesor/profesora

3 Separa las palabras y escribe los textos correctamente.

mellamoMaxtrabajoconniñosenunhospitalsoyenfermerosoyactivoypacienteymegustamuchomitrabajo

mellamomanuelasoycamareratrabajoenunrestauranteitalianomegustamuchotrabajarcongenteymegustatambiénhablaridiomasdiferentessoyhabladoraeindependiente

4 Escribe un párrafo sobre Fernando en español. Utiliza estos datos en inglés.

Ejemplo: Me llamo Fernando …

| Fernando |
| Cook |
| Likes job very much |
| Likes to work alone |
| Organized, creative and practical |

leer 5 Lee los textos. Empareja cada persona con la profesión correcta.
(There is one job too many.)

a Me llamo **Alicia**. Trabajo en una comisaría. Me gusta mucho trabajar en una comisaría. ¡No es nada aburrido! Tengo que llevar uniforme. Soy paciente y también soy independiente.

b Me llamo **Carlos**. Trabajo en unos estudios de Hollywood. Allí ruedo películas de acción o de aventura. Me gusta mucho trabajar en Hollywood. Soy muy activo y también soy fuerte. Conduzco todo tipo de vehículos. Me gusta trabajar solo.

c Me llamo **Pepe**. Trabajo en la cocina de un restaurante. Me gusta mucho trabajar en mi restaurante. La variedad es muy importante para mí y la calidad de la comida también. Soy práctico y también soy organizado.

d Me llamo **Antonia**. Trabajo en una oficina con mucha gente. Me gusta trabajar en una oficina y me gusta mucho mi trabajo porque es creativo. Soy muy creativa y también muy habladora.

conduzco = *I drive*

1 *Soy conductor especialista.*

2 *Soy camarera.*

3 *Soy diseñadora.*

4 *Soy cocinero.*

5 *Soy policía.*

escuchar 6 Escucha y escribe los datos para cada persona en inglés. (1–2)

1 What do they do?
2 Where do they work?
3 Do they like their work?
4 What sort of person are they?

hablar 7 Con tu compañero/a, haz entrevistas.

- ¿Cómo te llamas?
- Me llamo …
- ¿En qué trabajas?
- Soy …
- ¿Dónde trabajas?
- Trabajo …
- ¿Te gusta trabajar …?
- Sí, me gusta mucho.
- ¿Qué tipo de persona eres?
- Soy …

1 Jorge
- footballer
- work outside
- ♥ + outside
- active and independent

2 Isabel
- teacher
- in school
- ♥ + children
- creative and patient

5 El año pasado

escuchar 1 Escucha y lee el texto. Contesta a las preguntas en inglés.

1 Was Kirsty happy last year? Why?
2 Is Kirsty happy this year? Why?

Me llamo Kirsty. Soy escocesa. Soy una persona activa y organizada.

El año pasado trabajé de camarera en un restaurante de Ibiza. No me gustó mi jefe.

Puse las mesas, lavé los platos, limpié el restaurante después de la cena y también pasé la aspiradora. ¡Qué horror!

Gané mucho dinero pero no me gustó nada el trabajo. Fue aburrido.

Este año trabajo en un hotel y me gusta mucho. Es muy interesante. Mi jefe es muy guapo.

Soy recepcionista. Hablo con los clientes. Les hablo en inglés y español y les ayudo siempre.

leer 2 Lee el texto otra vez. Contesta a las preguntas en inglés.

Ejemplo: **1** Kirsty is active and organized.

1 What is Kirsty like?
2 What did she work as last year?
3 What jobs did she do?
4 How good was the pay?

5 What does she say about the work she did?
6 Where is she working this year?
7 What is she working as?
8 What are her duties?

leer 3 Lee el texto otra vez. Dos de estas frases son verdaderas. Escribe los números correctos.

Kirsty dice …
1 Soy inglesa.
2 El año pasado comí en un restaurante en Ibiza.
3 Lavé el coche y limpié la casa.
4 No me gustó el trabajo pero gané mucho dinero.
5 Este año trabajo como recepcionista.
6 Hablo inglés y mandarín.

Gramática

-ar verbs in the present		-ar verbs in the preterite	
trabaj**o**	*I work*	trabaj**é**	*I worked*
trabaj**as**	*you work*	trabaj**aste**	*you worked*
trabaj**a**	*he/she works*	trabaj**ó**	*he/she worked*

poner *(to put/lay)* is irregular in the preterite tense:
pongo   *I lay*   puse   *I laid*

Para saber más   página 132

leer 4 **Read these questions. Which of them are in the present tense (P) and which are in the preterite tense (PT)?**

1 ¿Dónde trabajaste el año pasado?
2 ¿Qué hiciste?
3 ¿Dónde trabajas este año?
4 ¿Qué haces?

5 ¿Te gustó?
6 ¿Ganaste mucho dinero?
7 ¿Te gusta?
8 ¿Ganas mucho dinero?

escuchar 5 Escucha y escribe la letra correcta. (1–8)

Ejemplo: **1** b

a Trabajé como recepcionista.
b Trabajé en un hotel en Madrid.
c Lavo los platos y paso la aspiradora. Es superaburrido…
d Me gustó mucho.
e No, no me gusta nada.
f Sí, gané mucho dinero.
g No, no gano mucho dinero.
h Trabajo en un restaurante.

hablar 6 Con tu compañero/a, pregunta y contesta.
(Use the verbs in the box below.)

● ¿Dónde trabajaste el año pasado?
● ¿Qué hiciste?
● ¿Te gustó?
● ¿Ganaste mucho dinero?
● ¿Dónde trabajas este año?
● ¿Qué haces?
● ¿Te gusta?
● ¿Ganas mucho dinero?

Past (preterite tense)

Worked in restaurant	trabajé
Washed dishes	lavé
Cleaned bar	limpié
Earned lots	gané
Didn't like it	no me gustó
Was boring	fue

Now (present tense)

Work in office	trabajo
Talk to people	hablo
Like it	me gusta
Is interesting	es
Earn	gano

escribir 7 Escribe tu texto del ejercicio 6.

Resumen

Unidad 1

I can

- talk about earning money — Lavo el coche. Paseo al perro. Pongo la mesa.
- ask someone what they do to earn money — ¿Qué haces para ganar dinero?
- say what I do with my money — Compro crédito para mi móvil. Ahorro.

Unidad 2

I can

- ask someone what they are like — ¿Qué tipo de persona eres?
- say what I am like — Soy creativo. Nunca soy impaciente.
- talk about what I'd like to do — Me gustaría viajar. No me gustaría trabajar solo.
- **G** form adjectives correctly — Soy muy activa y habladora.

Unidad 3

I can

- talk about using languages at work — Hablo mucho por teléfono y mando correos en francés y alemán.
- **G** say what I am going to do in the future — Voy a viajar. Voy a trabajar en un hotel.

Unidad 4

I can

- talk about jobs — Soy profesor/recepcionista/enfermero.
- ask someone about their job — ¿En qué trabajas?
- ask someone where they work — ¿Dónde trabajas?
- say why I like my job — Me gusta trabajar con niños. Me gusta trabajar al aire libre.
- **G** recognize masculine and feminine forms of jobs — profesor/profesora, enfermero/enfermera

Unidad 5

I can

- talk about work I have done — trabajé en un restaurante, lavé los platos, pasé la aspiradora
- **G** use two tenses together — El año pasado trabajé en un restaurante. Este año trabajo en un hotel.

1 Escucha y escribe las letras en el orden correcto. (1–6)

a

b *I speak English.*

c

d HOTEL

e *Ningún problema.*

f

 2 Listen again. Is each sentence in the present (P) or the preterite (PT)?

 3 Con tu compañero/a, pregunta y contesta.

- ● ¿Qué haces para ganar dinero?
- ■ Limpio la casa …
- ● ¿Qué haces con el dinero?
- ■ Compro …
- ● ¿Qué tipo de persona eres?
- ■ Soy …
- ● ¿Dónde te gustaría trabajar?
- ■ Me gustaría trabajar …

 4 Lee el texto. Completa las frases en inglés.

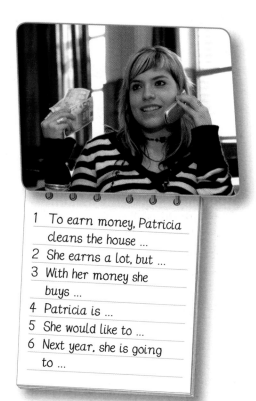

Trabajo mucho para ganar dinero. Limpio la casa y también pongo la mesa. Los fines de semana hago de canguro y paseo al perro. Gano mucho dinero pero no me gusta el trabajo. Con el dinero, compro revistas y crédito para mi móvil. Soy habladora. Soy bastante inteligente, también soy creativa y muy paciente. En el futuro me gustaría trabajar con niños. El año que viene voy a viajar por Asia para conocer otras culturas.

1 To earn money, Patricia cleans the house …
2 She earns a lot, but …
3 With her money she buys …
4 Patricia is …
5 She would like to …
6 Next year, she is going to …

 5 Escribe un párrafo sobre ti. Incluye los siguientes datos.

- • wash car and clean house to earn money
- • would like to work in open air
- • would like to work with people
- • going to travel
- • going to work in a hotel

Escucha y completa el currículum.

Currículum Vitae	
Información personal	
1 Apellido(s)	Martínez López
2 Nombre(s)	**a** …
3 Dirección	Calle **b** …
	c … 45003
4 Correo electrónico	**d** …@yahoo.es
5 Fecha de nacimiento	**e** … 1992
Experiencia profesional	
6 Puesto	**f** …
7 Actividades	**g** …
Aptitudes personales	
8 Personalidad	**h** …
9 Pasatiempos	**i** …

- Most Spanish people have two surnames, one from their father and one from their mother.
- In a Spanish address, you usually give the street name, <u>then</u> the house number, <u>then</u> the apartment number.

@ = *arroba*
1992 = *mil novecientos noventa y dos*

2 Lee el currículum. Eres Antonio. Con tu compañero/a, pregunta y contesta.

- ¿Cuál es tu nombre?
- ¿Cuáles son tus apellidos?
- ■ Me llamo …
- ¿Cuál es tu dirección?
- ■ Mi dirección es …
- ¿Cómo se escribe?
- ■ Se escribe …
- ¿Y tu correo electrónico?
- ■ Mi correo electrónico es …
- ¿Cuándo naciste?
- ■ Nací el …
- ¿En qué trabajaste el año pasado?
- ■ Trabajé como …
- ¿Qué hiciste?
- ■ Puse …
- ¿Qué tipo de persona eres?
- ■ Soy …
- ¿Qué haces en tu tiempo libre?
- ■ Juego al …

Currículum Vitae	
Información personal	
Apellido(s)	Barrera Rodríguez
Nombre(s)	Antonio Carlos
Dirección	Plaza Guzmán 57, 29480 Málaga
Correo electrónico	antcar58@yahoo.es
Fecha de nacimiento	5/9/1988
Experiencia profesional	
Puesto	camarero
Actividades	poner mesas, lavar los platos
Aptitudes personales	
Personalidad	práctico, hablador, independiente, inteligente
Pasatiempos	fútbol, tenis, idiomas

3 **Listen and read. Which job is Sofía applying for?**

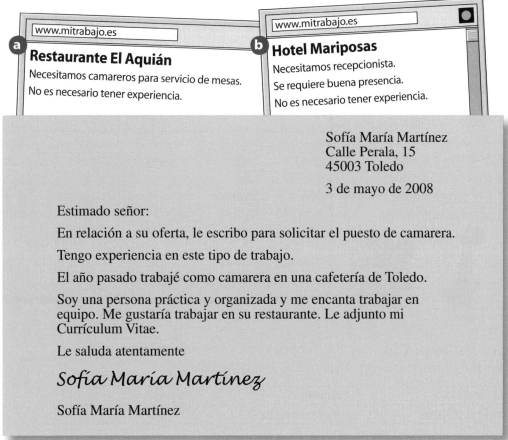

a www.mitrabajo.es

Restaurante El Aquián

Necesitamos camareros para servicio de mesas.
No es necesario tener experiencia.

b www.mitrabajo.es

Hotel Mariposas

Necesitamos recepcionista.
Se requiere buena presencia.
No es necesario tener experiencia.

Sofía María Martínez
Calle Perala, 15
45003 Toledo

3 de mayo de 2008

Estimado señor:

En relación a su oferta, le escribo para solicitar el puesto de camarera.

Tengo experiencia en este tipo de trabajo.

El año pasado trabajé como camarera en una cafetería de Toledo.

Soy una persona práctica y organizada y me encanta trabajar en equipo. Me gustaría trabajar en su restaurante. Le adjunto mi Currículum Vitae.

Le saluda atentamente

Sofía María Martínez

Sofía María Martínez

4 **Busca el equivalente en español de estas frases en la carta.**

Ejemplo: **1** Estimado señor

1 Dear Sir
2 In relation to your advert
3 I am writing to you to apply for the job of …

4 I have experience in this kind of work
5 I attach my CV.
6 Yours faithfully

5 **Escribe una carta de presentación para el puesto de recepcionista del ejercicio 3.**

Estimado señor:

En relación a su oferta, le escribo para solicitar el puesto de …

Tengo experiencia en este tipo de trabajo.

El año pasado trabajé como …

Soy …

Me gustaría …

Le adjunto mi Currículum Vitae.

Le saluda atentamente

THE CITY OF PORTSMOUTH GIRLS' SCHOOL
ST. MARY'S ROAD
PORTSMOUTH
PO1 5PF

Gramática

escribir 1 Use the grid to help you translate the sentences into Spanish.

Example: **1** Pongo la mesa.

❶ I lay the table.
❷ I do babysitting.
❸ You wash the car.
❹ He delivers newspapers.
❺ She lays the table.
❻ He walks the dog.
❼ Do you clean the house?
❽ She walks the dog.

-ar **lavar** *(to wash)*		-ir **repartir** *(to deliver)*	hacer *(to do/make)*	poner *(to put/lay)*
(I)	lav**o**	repart**o**	ha**go**	pon**go**
(you)	lav**as**	repart**es**	hac**es**	pon**es**
(he/she/it)	lav**a**	repart**e**	hac**e**	pon**e**
(we)	lav**amos**	repart**imos**	hac**emos**	pon**emos**
(you pl.)	lav**áis**	repart**ís**	hac**éis**	pon**éis**
(they)	lav**an**	repart**en**	hac**en**	pon**en**

limpi**ar** = *to clean*
pase**ar** = *to walk (the dog)*

leer 2 Read the texts. Copy out the table and put the adjectives in green into the correct column. Then fill in the other forms.

Masculino	Femenino	Inglés
independiente	independiente	independent

❶ Soy **independiente** como mi gato. Me encanta pasar tiempo con mi gato.
❷ Soy **creativo** pero **práctico**. Me interesa mucho el diseño.
❸ Soy bastante **paciente**. Quiero ser profesora.
❹ Soy **inteligente** y **organizada**. Me gusta mucho la informática. No me gustaría nada trabajar al aire libre.
❺ Soy muy **activa**. Tengo mucha energía. Me gustaría visitar muchos países.
❻ No soy muy **hablador**. No me gustaría trabajar con gente.
❼ Soy activo y **fuerte**.
❽ Soy muy habladora. No me gustaría nada trabajar **sola**.

leer 3 Read the text and find the following:

❶ eight verbs in the present tense
❷ one verb in the conditional
❸ two verbs in the near future tense
❹ three adjectives

Me llamo Polita. Soy española. Trabajo en un hotel en España.
Hablo bien español, francés e inglés. Trabajo principalmente con gente.
No me gustaría trabajar sola. Soy muy práctica y habladora.
Hago reservas para los clientes y soluciono problemas. Hablo mucho por teléfono y también mando correos en inglés, francés y español. A veces voy de excursión con mis clientes. El año que viene voy a viajar un poco y voy a estudiar alemán.

escribir 4 *Write a caption for each picture.*

Example: **1** Soy diseñadora.

leer 5 *Match the Spanish verbs in the past tense with their English translations.*

viajé

trabajé

estudié

me gustó

hablé

mandé

visité

puse

I liked

I laid

I travelled

I worked

I visited

I studied

I sent

I spoke

leer 6 *Read the sentences. Copy and fill in the grid with each letter in the correct column.*

	Pasado	Presente
1	a	

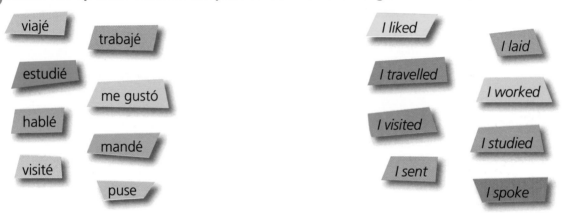

a **b** **c** **d** **e** **f** **g** **h**

1. El año pasado, **estudié** español en España y ahora **trabajo** en una cafetería, en Madrid.
2. Ahora **soy** recepcionista y **hablo** mucho por teléfono. El año pasado **viajé** mucho.
   Visité unos países muy interesantes.
3. El año pasado **trabajé** en una oficina, pero no me gustó mucho. Este año **estudio**
   francés, me encanta.
4. **Trabajo** en un restaurante y **me gusta** mucho. El año pasado **trabajé** en un hotel
   como camarero. **Me gustó** bastante.

leer 7 *Read the sentences in exercise 6 again and find the Spanish for the following.*

Example: **1** estudié

1. I studied
2. I am
3. I travelled
4. I liked
5. I worked
6. I speak
7. I visited
8. I like
9. I study
10. I work

Palabras

El dinero / *Money*

¿Qué haces para ganar dinero?	*What do you do to earn money?*
Hago de canguro.	*I babysit.*
Lavo el coche.	*I wash the car.*
Limpio la casa.	*I clean the house.*
Paseo al perro.	*I walk the dog.*
Paso la aspiradora.	*I do the vacuuming.*
Plancho la ropa.	*I do the ironing.*
Pongo la mesa.	*I lay the table.*
Reparto periódicos.	*I deliver papers.*
No hago nada.	*I do nothing.*
¿Qué haces con tu dinero?	*What do you do with your money?*
Compro …	*I buy …*
maquillaje	*make-up*
CDs o DVDs	*CDs or DVDs*
ropa	*clothes*
videojuegos	*videogames*
crédito para mi móvil	*credit for my mobile*
revistas	*magazines*
chocolate y caramelos	*chocolate and sweets*
(No) ahorro.	*I (don't) save.*
todos los días	*every day*
a veces	*sometimes*
los fines de semana	*at the weekend*

Soy … / *I'm …*

Soy …	*I'm …*
Nunca soy …	*I'm never …*
activo/a	*active*
creativo/a	*creative*
fuerte	*strong*
hablador(a)	*talkative*
independiente	*independent*
inteligente	*intelligent*
organizado/a	*organised*
paciente	*patient*
práctico/a	*practical*

Me gustaría … / *I'd like to …*

¿Qué te gustaría hacer?	*What would you like to do?*
Me gustaría trabajar …	*I'd like to work …*
No me gustaría trabajar …	*I wouldn't like to work …*
al aire libre	*in the open air*
con animales	*with animals*
con gente	*with people*
con niños	*with children*
en una oficina	*in an office*
solo/a	*alone*
Me gustaría viajar.	*I would like to travel.*
Me gustaría hacer …	*I would like to do …*
un trabajo creativo	*a creative job*
un trabajo manual	*a manual job*

Los idiomas / *Languages*

¿Qué idiomas hablas?	*Which languages do you speak?*
Hablo …	*I speak …*
español	*Spanish*
francés	*French*
inglés	*English*
alemán	*German*
Hablo por teléfono.	*I talk on the phone.*
Hago reservas.	*I make reservations.*
Soluciono problemas.	*I solve problems.*
Voy de excursión con mis clientes.	*I go on trips with my customers.*
Mando correos.	*I send emails.*
Hablo con …	*I talk to …*
los camareros	*the waiters*
la recepcionista	*the receptionist*
el cocinero	*the cook*
el servicio de limpieza	*the cleaning staff*

¿En qué trabajas? — *What's your job?*

Soy …	*I'm a(n) …*
camarero/a	*waiter/waitress*
cocinero/a	*cook, chef*
conductor especialista	*stunt driver*
diseñador(a)	*designer*
enfermero/a	*nurse*
futbolista	*footballer*
ingeniero/a	*engineer*
médico/a	*doctor*
policía	*police officer*
profesor(a)	*teacher*
recepcionista	*receptionist*
¿En qué trabajas?	*What's your job?*
¿Dónde trabajas?	*Where do you work?*
Trabajo …	*I work …*
en una comisaría	*in a police station*
en una oficina	*in an office*
en la cocina de un restaurante	*in a restaurant kitchen*
al aire libre	*outdoors*
¿Te gusta trabajar al aire libre?	*Do you like working outdoors?*
¿Qué tipo de persona eres?	*What sort of person are you?*

El año pasado — *Last year*

¿Dónde trabajaste el año pasado?	*Where did you work last year?*
Trabajé …	*I worked …*
¿Qué hiciste?	*What did you do?*
Lavé los platos.	*I washed the dishes.*
Limpié.	*I cleaned.*
¿Te gustó?	*Did you like it?*
(No) me gustó.	*I liked (didn't like) it.*
¿Ganaste mucho dinero?	*Did you earn a lot of money?*
Gané …	*I earned …*

Ahora — *Now*

¿Dónde trabajas este año?	*Where do you work this year?*
Trabajo …	*I work …*
¿Qué haces?	*What do you do?*
Lavo los platos.	*I wash the dishes.*
Limpio.	*I clean.*
¿Te gusta?	*Do you like it?*
(No) me gusta.	*I (don't) like it.*
¿Ganas mucho dinero?	*Do you earn a lot of money?*
Gano …	*I earn …*

Palabras muy útiles — *Very useful words*

con	*with*
ahora	*now*
este año	*this year*
el año que viene	*next year*
el año pasado	*last year*

Estrategia

Checking the endings of words

There are two groups of words in this module that change depending on whether they refer to a man or a woman.

- job titles
- adjectives to describe personality

To learn the ending properly and help you remember to use them, categorise them into three groups:

male	both	female
organizado creativo	fuerte independiente	organizada creativa

Copy and finish off filling in these circles for adjectives, then create a second set of circles for jobs. They will help you to talk about people and jobs using correct Spanish!

1 El mundo hispano

 1 Escucha. Copia y rellena la tabla. (1–3)

		Países donde se habla español
1	Norteamérica	
2	Centroamérica	
3	Sudamérica	

 2 Escucha. Copia y rellena la tabla para cada país. (1–4)

	País	Capital
1	Venezuela	Caracas

País	Capital
México	Tegucigalpa
Honduras	Ciudad de México
Venezuela	Buenos Aires
Argentina	Caracas

¿Cómo se llama la capital de …?

La capital de … se llama …

 3 Haz preguntas sobre los países del ejercicio 2.

● ¿Cómo se llama la capital de <u>Venezuela</u>?
■ La capital de <u>Venezuela</u> se llama …

" Make sure you pronounce the countries in a Spanish way! Listen and repeat their names:

México, Honduras, Venezuela, Argentina "

Estados Unidos

Norteamérica

Honduras

Cuba

México

Nicaragua

República Dominicana

Guatemala

Puerto Rico

El Salvador

Panamá   **Caribe**

Centroamérica

Costa Rica

Venezuela

Colombia

Ecuador

El río Amazonas

Sudamérica

La cordillera de los Andes

Perú

Chile

Paraguay

Bolivia

Uruguay

Argentina

escuchar 4 Escucha y lee. Luego copia y rellena la tabla.

Country	Capital	Geographical features	Products

montañas

un desierto

Los productos principales son …

volcanes

la selva amazónica

la fruta

el café

el río Amazonas

una llanura

la caña de azúcar

el petróleo

Mi viaje a Sudamérica fue estupendo. Fui con unos amigos. Fuimos a Perú en avión y ¡lo pasamos bomba! Perú está en Sudamérica, en la costa.

Primero fuimos a Lima, la capital de Perú. Lima es muy interesante. Está en la costa frente al océano Pacífico. Desde Lima fuimos de excursión. La geografía de Perú es estupenda. En Perú están el río Amazonas, la selva amazónica, la llanura y el desierto. Luego fuimos a las montañas, a los Andes. También visitamos el valle de los volcanes.

Los productos principales de Perú son la fruta, el café, la caña de azúcar y el petróleo.

Ser describes something ongoing or permanent. *La capital de Perú **es** Lima.*
Estar describes location or something temporary. *Lima **está** en Perú.*

to be	ser	estar
I am	soy	estoy
you are	eres	estás
he/she/it is	es	está
we are	somos	estamos
you (plural) are	sois	estáis
they are	son	están

escribir 5 Elige un país y haz un póster. Utiliza los datos siguientes.

País	Chile	México
Capital	Santiago	Ciudad de México
Geografía	montañas, llanura, desierto	desierto, volcanes, llanura
Productos	fruta, caña de azúcar, café	fruta, café

Este país se llama …
Está en (Sudamérica).
(No) Está en la costa.
La capital se llama …
La geografía es muy interesante. Hay …
Los productos principales son …

Learning more about Central and South America
Listening for gist and detail

hablar 1 Juega con otras tres personas.

13 El canal de Panamá pasa
a del océano Pacífico al océano Atlántico
b del mar Mediterráneo al océano Atlántico

14 El Popocatépetl es
a un océano
b un volcán activo

15 FIN

12 Centroamérica tiene
a siete países
b ocho países

11 Machu Picchu es una ciudad
a inca
b azteca

10

7

8 Las montañas que están en Sudamérica se llaman
a los Pirineos
b los Andes

9

6

5 En las Islas Galápagos hay
a muchas tortugas
b muchos conejos

4 El río más largo del continente se llama
a el río Orinoco
b el río Amazonas

1 Empieza aquí.

2 Sudamérica tiene
a doce países
b trece países
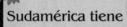

3 La montaña más alta del continente se llama
a el Aconcagua
b el Monte Everest

Respuestas
2a 3a 4b 5a 9b
11a 12a 13a 14b

Try to use these expressions in Spanish as you play the game. Listen and repeat them to make sure you are saying them correctly.

Te toca a ti. = *Your turn.*
Me toca a mí. = *My turn.*
¡Muy bien! = *Well done!*
No. Prueba otra vez. = *No. Try again.*
¡He ganado! = *I've won!*
Lo siento, mala suerte. = *Sorry. Bad luck.*

escribir 2 Escribe tus respuestas para ejercicio 1. Escribe frases.

Ejemplo: **1** Sudamérica tiene doce países.

3 Escucha y pon estos temas en el orden correcto.

(There is one topic too many.)

Ejemplo: c, ...

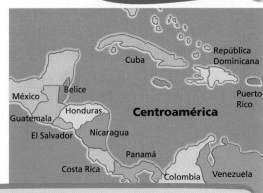

República Dominicana
Cuba
México
Belice
Puerto Rico
Guatemala
Honduras
Centroamérica
El Salvador
Nicaragua
Panamá
Costa Rica
Colombia
Venezuela

a Details of her trip last year

b The weather

c Countries of Central America

d The landscape

e People

f Animals

When you are listening for gist, try to:
● decide roughly what the text is about.
● predict what sort of words you might hear for each of the topics in exercise 3.
● listen to each section again to get more detail.

4 Escucha otra vez y escribe las letras correctas.

Ejemplo: **1** c, ...

1 the order in which she mentions these seven countries
  a Panama   **e** Costa Rica
  b Belize   **f** El Salvador
  c Guatemala **g** Nicaragua
  d Honduras

2 what she ate on the plane

  a
  b
  c

3 what type of weather she mentions

  a
  b
  c

4 which geographical features she mentions

  a
  b
  c

5 which animals she mentions

  a
  b
  c
  d

5 Haz una presentación sobre Centroamérica y Sudamérica.

● Sudamérica tiene ... países. Son ...
● Centroamérica tiene ... países. Son ...
● En verano ... En invierno ... *(describe the weather)*
● La geografía es muy interesante. Hay ...
● Hay muchos animales, por ejemplo ...

3 Mi vida diaria

- Describing daily routine
- Using clock times and reflexive verbs

1 Empareja los dibujos con las frases. Escucha y comprueba tus respuestas.

a b c d e f g h

1 Son las cuatro.	**5** Son las once y cuarto.
2 Son las tres y media.	**6** Son las siete y diez.
3 Son las diez menos cuarto.	**7** Es la una.
4 Son las doce y veinte.	**8** Son las seis menos veinte.

2 Escucha y lee. (a–g)

> me levanto = *I get up*
> la madrugada = *very early morning*
> me acuesto = *I go to bed*

a Me llamo Magali. Tengo catorce años. Soy de Colombia.

b No voy al instituto. Trabajo en una plantación de flores.

c Me levanto muy temprano, a las cuatro de la madrugada.

d Salgo de casa a las cuatro y media. Camino una hora hasta la estación de autobuses.

e Después cojo el autobús. El viaje dura cuarenta y cinco minutos.

f Empiezo a trabajar a las seis y media de la mañana.

g Cada día trabajo ocho horas. Termino a las dos y media de la tarde. Me acuesto a las ocho y media.

ZONA CULTURA

Magali has a very hard life, but most children in Colombia do not live in such poverty.

87% go to primary school and 93% of children aged 15 can read. There is, however, a big gap between rich and poor in Colombia.

3 Copia y completa el texto.

Magali is **(1)** 14 years old. She lives in **(2)** ___. She doesn't go to **(3)** ___. She works on a **(4)** ___ plantation. She gets up at **(5)** ___. She leaves home at **(6)** ___ and walks for one **(7)** ___ to catch the bus. The bus journey takes **(8)** ___. She starts work at **(9)** ___ and finishes at **(10)** ___. She goes to bed at **(11)** ___.

4 Copia las preguntas y emparéjalas con las respuestas.

Ejemplo: **1** ¿Cómo te llamas?
d Me llamo …

1 ¿Cómo te llamas?
2 ¿Cuántos años tienes?
3 ¿De dónde eres?
4 ¿En qué trabajas?
5 ¿A qué hora te levantas?
6 ¿A qué hora sales de casa?
7 ¿A qué hora empiezas a trabajar?
8 ¿A qué hora terminas?
9 ¿A qué hora te acuestas?

a Normalmente, me acuesto …
b Trabajo en una plantación …
c Empiezo a las …
d Me llamo …
e Termino a las …
f Salgo de casa a las …
g Me levanto a las …
h Tengo …
i Soy de …

5 Escucha y completa las respuestas del ejercicio 4.

Ejemplo: **1** Me llamo Héctor.

6 Con tu compañero/a, haz preguntas y contesta por Carlos.

" Make a clear difference in sound between **l** and **ll**. Listen and practise these words.

me **l**evanto
me **ll**amo
"

Gramática

Reflexive verbs describe an action you do to yourself, e.g. **levantarse**, *to get (yourself) up*.

me	levanto	*I get up*
te	levantas	*you get up*
se	levanta	*he/she gets up*

Can you spot the two other reflexive verbs in the questions and answers in exercise 4?

Para saber más   página 000

- 10 años   Carlos
- Nicaragua
- una plantación de cacao   • 6:00

- 5:00   • 17:00

- 5:30   • 21:00

Mini-test

I can …
- talk about Spanish-speaking countries and their capitals
- talk about the geographical features
- describe the daily routine of a working child in South America
- **G** use reflexive verbs

Escucha y escribe la letra correcta. (1–7)

Ejemplo: **1** b

> Me llamo Diego. Vivo con mi familia en Ciudad de México.

a Hay demasiado tráfico.

b Hay mucha contaminación.

c Hay mucha basura.

d Hay muchas fábricas.

e El tráfico causa mucho ruido.

f Mucha gente usa el carro todos los días.

g No hay espacios verdes.

In Latin-American Spanish, the words for certain things are different:

Latin America	Spain	
carro	coche	*car*
camión	autobús	*bus*
computadora	ordenador	*computer*
lindo	bonito	*nice*

leer 2 **Copia y completa el texto con las palabras del cuadro.**
Luego lee en voz alta con tu compañero/a.

basura	familia	ruido	fábricas	contaminación	tráfico	carro

Me llamo Diego. Vivo con mi ⁽¹⁾ en Ciudad de México. En nuestra ciudad hay mucha

⁽²⁾ 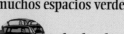. Hay muchas ⁽³⁾ y no hay muchos espacios verdes. También

hay mucho ⁽⁴⁾ . Mucha gente usa el ⁽⁵⁾ todos los días. Hay mucho

⁽⁶⁾ también. En las calles hay mucha ⁽⁷⁾ , porque la gente no recicla.

nuestra = *our*

escribir 3 **Escribe un párrafo sobre tu región.**

Ejemplo: Vivo en … En mi región (no) hay muchos problemas con el medio ambiente.
Por ejemplo … También …

escuchar 4 Empareja los dibujos con las frases correctas.
Escucha y comprueba tus respuestas.

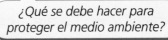
¿Qué se debe hacer para proteger el medio ambiente?

Ejemplo: **1** c

a Se debe comprar productos verdes.

b Se debe reciclar papel y vidrio.

c Se debe reducir la contaminación.

d Se debe usar más el transporte público.

e Se debe apagar la luz y utilizar menos energía.

f Se debe plantar más árboles.

g No se debe tirar basura al suelo.

escuchar 5 Escucha. Copia y rellena la tabla en inglés. (1–4)

	Problem	Solution(s)
1	too much traffic,	use public transport
2		
3		
4		

hablar 6 Con tu compañero/a, pregunta y contesta.

● ¿Qué se debe hacer para proteger el medio ambiente?
■ Se debe <u>comprar productos verdes</u> y también se debe <u>apagar la luz</u>.

1   **2**   **3**   **4**

leer 7 Lee el texto y escribe los números de las tres frases correctas.

sucias = *dirty*
motos = *motorbikes*
por eso = *that is why*
debería = *one should*

Me llamo Aymara. Vivo en Caracas, la capital de Venezuela. La contaminación en nuestra ciudad es un problema muy grande.
Las calles están sucias porque la gente tira basura al suelo. Hay mucho tráfico: hay carros, camiones y también motos y por eso hay mucho ruido.
Pero en casa, reciclo papel y vidrio. También compro productos verdes, pero debería apagar la luz en casa. Y mi madre usa su carro todos los días; debería usar más el transporte público.

1 La contaminación en Caracas no es un problema muy grande.
2 Mucha gente tira basura al suelo.
3 Hay mucho tráfico y por eso hay mucho ruido.
4 Aymara no recicla mucho.
5 Aymara compra productos verdes.
6 La madre de Aymara no debería usar más el transporte público.

escuchar 1 Escucha y lee. Escribe tres datos para cada persona en inglés.

chabola = *shack, shanty town*

Diego Maradona

Me llamo Diego Maradona. Soy de Argentina.
Nací en Buenos Aires, en 1960.
Soy muy bajo y soy bastante hablador.
Empecé a jugar al fútbol con mis amigos en un barrio de chabolas.
En 1977 recibí el premio al mejor jugador argentino.
En 1982 firmé un contrato con el Barcelona y en 1984 con el Nápoles.
En 1991 me acusaron de tráfico de drogas.
En 1992 firmé un contrato con el Sevilla.
En 1997 me retiré del fútbol.
Tuve problemas de salud, también tomé drogas.
Tuve que cambiar mi vida.
Ahora vivo con mis padres.
Tengo dos hijas, Dalma y Giannina.
Me gusta mucho ver la televisión e ir de vacaciones a Cuba.
Me encanta el fútbol, es mi pasión.

Shakira

Me llamo Shakira. Soy de Colombia.
Nací en Barranquilla el 2 de febrero de 1977.
Mi nombre significa 'mujer llena de gracia'.
Empecé a cantar de niña.
Con trece años firmé un contrato con Sony.
Mi primer álbum se llamó *Magia*.
En 2001 gané un Grammy como mejor cantante pop latina.
Escribo canciones en español y en inglés.
Me encanta el rock y el pop y también me gusta mucho bailar.
Odio la música comercial.
Hablo portugués, árabe, italiano, español e inglés.
Vivo en las Bahamas.
Tengo cinco hermanos y tres hermanas.

leer 2 Contesta a las preguntas.

Who …

1 is short and quite talkative?
2 lives in the Bahamas?
3 played in Barcelona?
4 lives with their parents?
5 has five brothers and three sisters?
6 started to sing as a child?
7 had health problems?
8 writes in Spanish and English?
9 took drugs?

leer 3 Busca los verbos en español en los textos.

1 I was born	6 I won	11 I write
2 I received	7 I began	12 I like
3 I signed	8 I had	13 I love
4 I retired	9 I made	14 I hate
5 I took	10 I live	15 I speak

Gramática

Present tense

The 'I' form mostly ends in **-o**:

me llamo	*I am called*
hablo	*I speak*
vivo	*I live*
tengo	*I have*

gustar/encantar

me gusta	*I like …*
me gusta**n** *(plural)*	
me encanta	*I love …*
me encanta**n** *(plural)*	

Some verbs are irregular:

soy	*I am*

Para saber más   **página xx**

Gramática

Preterite tense

-ar verbs: the 'I' form ends in **-é**.

(firmar) firm**é**	*I signed*
(ganar) gan**é**	*I won*
(retirarse) me retir**é**	*I retired*

-er and **-ir** verbs: the 'I' form ends in **-í**.

(nacer) nac**í**	*I was born*
(recibir) recib**í**	*I received*

Some verbs are irregular

(tener) tuve	*I had*
(hacer) hice	*I did/made*

Para saber más   **página xx**

---

hablar **4** **Pretend you are Gael García Bernal. Describe yourself to your partner.**

Gael García Bernal.

México	
Guadalajara, el 30 de noviembre de 1978	
con 1 año	
telenovelas	
Amores perros, en 2000	
español, inglés, francés e italiano.	
Diarios de motocicleta	
el fútbol	
leer y bailar salsa	
las preguntas sobre mi vida privada.	

Me llamo …
Soy de …
Nací en … el …
Empecé a actuar …
Trabajé en …
Mi primera gran película fue …
Hablo …
En 2004 hice la película …
Me encanta …
Me gusta …
Odio/No me gusta nada …

You say years in Spanish like this:
1978   mil novecientos **setenta y ocho**
2000   dos mil
2004   dos mil **cuatro**

---

escribir **5** **Eres Gael García Bernal. Escribe sobre tu vida.**

> *Ejemplo:* Me llamo Gael …

Resumen

Unidad 1

I can

- name some Spanish-speaking countries — Nicaragua, Ecuador, Venezuela, …
- give information about one of those countries — Venezuela está en Sudamérica.
  La capital se llama Caracas.
- give information about the country's products — Los productos principales son petróleo y fruta.
- give information about the geography — Hay montañas, una llanura, un desierto.
- **G** use **ser** and **estar** — **Es** muy interesante. **Está** en la costa.

Unidad 2

I can

- talk about the number of countries in South America — Sudamérica tiene trece países.
- talk about geographical features — El río más largo del continente se llama el río Amazonas. Las montañas se llaman los Andes.
- talk about wildlife — Hay muchas tortugas.
- talk about sites of interest — Machu Picchu es una ciudad inca.

Unidad 3

I can

- talk from the point of view of a teenager in South America — Me llamo … Soy de Colombia.
- say where I work — Trabajo en una plantación de flores.
- say when I start and finish work — Empiezo a las seis y media de la mañana. Termino a las cinco de la tarde.
- ask someone about their working conditions — ¿En qué trabajas? ¿A qué hora te levantas?
- **G** use reflexive verbs — Me levanto a las cuatro y media. Me acuesto a las nueve.

Unidad 4

I can

- talk about environmental problems — Hay mucha contaminación.
- say what we should do — Se debe reciclar papel y vidrio.
- **G** use **se debe** + *infinitive* — Se debe usar más el transporte público.

Unidad 5

I can

- give personal details from the point of view of a celebrity — Me llamo Shakira. Soy de Colombia.
- say what I like — Me encanta el fútbol.
- say what I don't like — Odio la música comercial.
- **G** use the 'I' form of the preterite to talk about a career — Nací en 1978. Empecé a cantar con … años.

Escucha. Copia y rellena la tabla para los tres países. (1–3)

	País	Capital	Geografía	Productos
1				
2				
3				

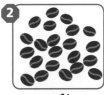 **Con tu compañero/a, pregunta y contesta.**

- ¿De dónde eres?
- ¿En qué trabajas?
- ¿A qué hora te levantas?
- ¿A qué hora sales de casa?
- ¿A qué hora empiezas?
- ¿A qué hora terminas?
- ¿A qué hora te acuestas?

- Soy de …
- Trabajo en …
- Me levanto …
- Salgo …
- Empiezo …
- Termino …
- Me acuesto …

1

2 café

3 5:00

4 5:30

5 6:00

6 18:00

7 21:00

 Lee el texto. Contesta a las preguntas en inglés.

Me llamo Jorge. Vivo en Buenos Aires en Argentina.
La contaminación en nuestra ciudad no es un problema muy grande.
Por lo general, la gente no tira mucha basura al suelo, pero hay
muchos carros en el centro y el tráfico causa mucho ruido en la ciudad.
Es muy importante proteger el medio ambiente. Se debe plantar más
árboles en la ciudad. Se debe comprar productos verdes y se debe
reciclar papel y vidrio. También se debe usar más el transporte público.
¡Y se debe apagar la luz!

Jorge

1 What does Jorge say about pollution in Buenos Aires?
2 What two problems does Buenos Aires have?
3 Name five things Jorge says it is important to do to protect the environment.

4 Describe la situación en el Reino Unido. ¿Qué se debe hacer para proteger el medio ambiente?

1 Empareja las frases en español y inglés.

Ejemplo: **1** d

El sello de comercio justo significa:

1 Un salario digno para los productores del Sur
2 Una mejora de las condiciones de trabajo de los productores del Sur
3 Una mejora de las condiciones de vida de los productores del Sur
4 La garantía del origen 'justo' de los productos
5 Una especial atención a la calidad de los productos

a Improved living conditions for producers in the South
b Special attention given to the quality of the product
c Improved working conditions for producers in the South
d A fair salary for producers in the South
e The guarantee that products are produced fairly

Fairtrade (comercio justo) is an organization which helps individual producers of coffee, cocoa beans or fruit to get a fair price for their goods in the global market. The logo shows you that a fair price is being paid to the producers.

Guarantees a **better deal** for Third World Producers ® FAIRTRADE

2 Escucha y lee. Copia y rellena la tabla en inglés.

Eufrasia's life last year	Eufrasia's life this year

la ayuda = *help*
la calidad = *quality*

a BOLIVIA

Me llamo Eufrasia. **Vivo** en Bolivia. **Soy** agricultora.

b El año pasado **planté** arroz y bananas pero me **dieron** muy poco dinero por ellos.

c El año pasado sólo **comí** arroz.

d Este año **voy a plantar** cacao. Con la ayuda de 'comercio justo', el precio **es** más justo y la calidad del cacao es mejor.

e Además las condiciones de vida **son** mejores. Mis hijos **pueden** ir al colegio y de vez en cuando comen carne.

f Y **vamos a tener** un hospital en el pueblo.

3 Contesta a las preguntas en inglés.

Ejemplo: **1** Eufrasia lives in Bolivia.

1 Where does Eufrasia live?
2 What job does she do?
3 What was the only thing she ate for a whole year?
4 Who has helped her get a better price?
5 What do her children eat now?
6 What can her children do now?
7 What does she hope to see in her village in the future?

 4 Copia la tabla. Pon los verbos del texto del ejercicio 2 en la columna correcta.

Preterite	Present	Near future
	me llamo = I'm called	

 5 Con tu compañero/a, pregunta y contesta.

Salvador

● ¿Cómo te llamas?

■ Me llamo Salvador

● ¿Qué plantaste el año pasado?

■ Soy de … Guatemala

● ¿De dónde eres?

■ El año pasado cultivé

● ¿Cuánto dinero te dieron?

■ Mi dieron 👎 dinero.

● ¿Qué cultivas este año?

■ Ahora cultivo

● ¿Qué van a hacer tus hijos el año que viene?

■ El año que viene, mis hijos …

6 Haz un póster y explica el comercio justo.

Guarantees a **better deal** for Third World Producers FAIRTRADE ®

Comercio justo quiere decir …

un salario digno, …

Gramática

1 **Choose the correct verb to complete the sentences.**

Example: **1** Soy bajo.

1 **Estoy / Soy** bajo.

2 Caracas **está / es** en Venezuela.

3 ¡Hola! ¿Cómo **estás / eres**?**Soy / Estoy** bien.

4 Cancún **está / es** en México.

5 Cancún **es / está** muy interesante.

6 Cancún **es / está** en la costa.

2 **Unjumble these questions, then write a reply to each using verbs from the box.**

Example: **1** ¿Cómo te llamas? Me llamo …

1 ¿Cómo llamas? te   **2** años ¿Cuántos tienes?

3 dónde ¿De eres?   **4** qué ¿A te hora levantas?

5 sales ¿A de qué casa? hora   **6** hora te qué acuestas? ¿A

me acuesto	me llamo	salgo	me levanto	tengo	soy

3 **Fill in the inkspots to apply the same pattern as for levantarse to the verbs acostarse and llamarse. Then write the English.**

Example: **1** me acuesto *I go to bed*

1 ⬛ acuesto

2 me llam⬛

3 te acuest⬛

4 ⬛ llamas

5 se llam⬛

6 ⬛ acuesta

> Reflexive verbs describe an action which you do to yourself, e.g. **levantarse**, *to get (yourself) up.*
>
> **me** levant**o**   *I get up*
> **te** levant**as**   *you get up*
> **se** levant**a**   *he/she gets up*

4 **Translate these sentences into Spanish.**

Example: 1 Para proteger el medio ambiente, se debe reciclar papel y vidrio.

In order to protect the environment …

1 … we must recycle paper and glass.   **2** … we must reduce pollution.

3 … we must use public transport more.   **4** … we must drop litter.

5 … we must turn off the light.   **6** … we must buy green products.

5 **Choose the correct word to complete the sentences.**

Example: 1 En Lima hay mucha contaminación.

1 En Lima hay **mucho / mucha** contaminación.
2 Hay **muchos / muchas** fábricas.
3 También hay **mucho / mucha** tráfico.
4 Hay **muchos / muchas** carros.
5 También hay **mucho / mucha** ruido.
6 La gente no recicla **mucho / mucha**.

> **mucho/mucha/muchos/muchas** *(a lot of)* is an adjective and is followed by a noun with which it agrees.
>
> | Singular | | Plural | |
> |---|---|---|---|
> | Masculine | Feminine | Masculine | Feminine |
> | mucho | mucha | muchos | muchas |
>
> El tráfico causa mucho ruido.   *The traffic causes a lot of noise.*
> Hay mucha basura.   *There's a lot of rubbish.*
>
> **Mucho** can also be an adverb *(a lot, much)*. In this case it doesn't change.
>
> La gente no recicla mucho.   *People don't recycle much.*
> No uso mucho el carro.   *I don't use the car much.*

6 **Copy out the text and fill in the gaps with verbs from the box. Write down whether the verb is in the present or the preterite tense.**

(1) Nací en Ciudad de México el 21 de febrero de 1975.
(2) _____ en Los Ángeles.
(3) _____ canciones en inglés.
(4) _____ el rap y el pop y me gusta bailar.
No me gusta nada la música clásica.
En 2000 **(5)** _____ un contrato con Sony.
En 2006 **(6)** _____ un Grammy a la mejor cantante.
(7) _____ español e inglés.
(8) _____ un hermano y dos hermanas

| gané | ~~nací~~ | firmé | tengo | hablo | me encanta | escribo | vivo |

Palabras

Hispanoamérica	**Latin America**
El Caribe	*The Caribbean*
Centroamérica	*Central America*
Norteamérica	*North America*
Sudamérica	*South America*
Argentina	*Argentina*
Bolivia	*Bolivia*
Chile	*Chile*
Colombia	*Colombia*
Costa Rica	*Costa Rica*
Cuba	*Cuba*
Ecuador	*Ecuador*
Guatemala	*Guatemala*
Honduras	*Honduras*
México	*Mexico*
Nicaragua	*Nicaragua*
Panamá	*Panama*
Paraguay	*Paraguay*
Perú	*Peru*
Puerto Rico	*Puerto Rico*
República Dominicana	*Dominican Republic*
El Salvador	*El Salvador*
Uruguay	*Uruguay*
Venezuela	*Venezuela*
Este país se llama …	*This country is called …*
Está en …	*It is in …*
¿Cómo se llama la capital de …?	*What is the capital of … called?*
La capital se llama …	*The capital is called …*

La geografía	**The geography**
Hay …	*There is/are …*
montañas	*mountains*
volcanes	*volcanoes*
un desierto	*a desert*
una llanura	*a plain*
el río Amazonas	*the River Amazon*
la selva amazónica	*the Amazonian forest/ jungle*
La geografía es …	*The geography is …*
Los productos principales son …	*The main products are …*
el café	*coffee*

el petróleo	*oil/petroleum*
la caña de azúcar	*sugar cane*
la fruta	*fruit*

¿Qué hora es?	**What time is it?**
Es la una.	*It's one o'clock.*
Son las dos.	*It's two o'clock.*
Son las dos y cuarto.	*It's quarter past two.*
Son las dos y media.	*It's half past two.*
Son las tres menos veinte.	*It's twenty to three.*
Son las tres menos cuarto.	*It's quarter to three.*

La vida diaria	**Daily life**
¿Cómo te llamas?	*What's your name?*
Me llamo …	*My name is …*
¿Cuántos años tienes?	*How old are you?*
Tengo … años.	*I'm … years old.*
¿De dónde eres?	*Where are you from?*
Soy de …	*I'm from …*
¿En qué trabajas?	*What work do you do?*
Trabajo en …	*I work in …*
¿A qué hora …	*What time …*
te levantas?	*do you get up?*
sales de casa?	*do you leave home?*
empiezas a trabajar?	*do you start work?*
terminas?	*do you finish?*
te acuestas?	*do you go to bed?*
Me levanto …	*I get up …*
Salgo de casa …	*I leave home …*
Empiezo …	*I start …*
Termino …	*I finish …*
Me acuesto …	*I go to bed …*

El medio ambiente	The environment
Hay …	There's …
demasiado tráfico	too much traffic
mucha basura	a lot of rubbish
mucha contaminación	a lot of pollution
muchas fábricas	a lot of factories
No hay espacios verdes.	There are no green spaces.
El tráfico causa mucho ruido.	The traffic makes a lot of noise.
Mucha gente usa el carro todos los días.	A lot of people use the car every day.
¿Qué se debe hacer para proteger el medio ambiente?	What do we have to do to protect the environment?
Se debe …	We have to …
apagar la luz	turn off the light
comprar productos verdes	buy green products
plantar más árboles	plant more trees
reciclar papel y vidrio	recycle paper and glass
reducir la contaminación	reduce pollution
usar más el transporte público	use public transport more
utilizar menos energía	use less energy
No se debe …	We mustn't …
tirar basura al suelo	drop litter

Los famosos	Celebrities
Nací en … el …	I was born in … on …
Empecé a actuar …	I started to act …
Empecé a cantar …	I started to sing …
Empecé a jugar al fútbol …	I started to play football …
… con ocho años.	… at eight years old.
Mi primera película fue …	My first film was …
Hice la película …	I made the film …
Firmé un contrato.	I signed a contract.
Gané un Grammy.	I won a Grammy.
Tuve problemas de salud.	I had health problems.

Tuve que cambiar mi vida.	I had to change my life.
Ahora vivo en …	Now I live in …
Ahora vivo con …	Now I live with …
Tengo dos hijas.	I have two daughters.
Tengo un hermano.	I have one brother.
Hablo …	I speak …
Me encanta …	I love …
Me gusta …	I like …
Odio …	I hate …

Palabras muy útiles	Very useful words
mucho	a lot
mucho(s)/mucha(s) …	a lot of …
muy	very
más	more
menos	less

Estrategia

Extending your answers

Look at these two answers.

Hay mucha basura.

(1) En mi región hay mucha basura. **(2)** Mi ciudad está muy sucia. **(3)** No me gusta nada. **(4)** Se debe reciclar papel y vidrio.

Get into the habit of showing off what you know:
1 Say something.
2 Add something.
3 Give an opinion.
4 Say what should be done.

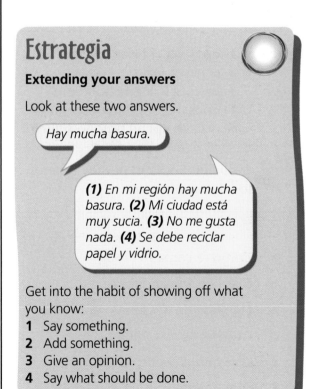

leer

1 **Lee los perfiles y contesta a las preguntas.**

(Which penfriend would you choose for yourself?)

Ejemplo: 1 Carolina

---

www.amigossinfronteras.es   ◉

**¡Hola! ¿Te gusta mandar mensajes y viajar? ¿Quieres tener un amigo español?
Este sitio web puede ayudarte ...**

14 años   **Juan**
Soy práctico y organizado. Nunca soy
perezoso.
Me gusta chatear y jugar al futbolín.
Me encantan las películas de ciencia-
ficción. *Matrix* es mi película favorita.
Me gusta el hip-hop y el flamenco.

15 años   **Isabel**
Soy creativa y habladora.
Me gusta salir con mis amigas, ir de
compras y mandar mensajes.
Me encantan las comedias.
Me gusta la música latina. Toco la guitarra en un grupo
y también canto. Es mi pasión.

14 años   **Jorge**
Soy independiente y a veces
impaciente, ¡pero muy divertido!
Me gusta navegar por internet y jugar
con el ordenador.
Me encantan las películas de artes marciales
porque son divertidas y emocionantes.
Me gusta la música electrónica y mi grupo favorito
es Hot Chip.

14 años   **Carolina**
Soy paciente y muy habladora.
Me gusta ir al cine. Voy a clases de
natación dos veces a la semana.
Me gustan mucho las películas
románticas. Mi actor favorito es Gael García
Bernal. Es guapísimo.
Me gusta la música clásica.

Who ...
1 does sport twice a week?
2 is never lazy?
3 loves science-fiction films?
4 does a lot on their computer?
5 likes to spend time with their friends?

6 likes classical music?
7 is not always patient?
8 plays table football?
9 plays an instrument?
10 likes romantic films?

escuchar

2 **Escucha. Copia el perfil y rellena
los datos correctos.**

---

www.amigossinfronteras.es/pablo   ◉

a ¿Cómo te llamas?   Pablo

b ¿Cuántos años tienes?

c ¿Qué tipo de persona eres?

d ¿Qué haces en tu tiempo libre?

e ¿Qué tipo de películas te gustan?

f ¿Qué tipo de música te gusta?

---

hablar

3 **Con tu compañero/a, pregunta y
contesta.**

(Use the questions from exercise 2.)

● ¿Cómo te llamas?
■ Me llamo ...

Try to add detail to your answers:
Nunca soy ...
Mi actor favorito es ...
Mi película favorita es ...
Mi grupo favorito es ...

---

escuchar 4 Escucha y lee. Empareja los párrafos con las fotos.

Ejemplo: **a** 3

padrastro = *stepfather*

Norte
Oeste ← → Este
Sur

a ¡Querido Liam!
Me presento. Soy tu nuevo amigo español de intercambio. **Tengo** quince años y **vivo en** Bermeo. **Vivo con** mi madre, mi padrastro y mi hermana. **Soy** hablador pero a veces perezoso. **Me encanta** navegar por internet y me gusta mucho el rap.

b Bermeo **está** en el País Vasco, en el norte de España. Está en la costa.

c **Hablo** español, inglés y también euskera. El euskera es el idioma tradicional del País Vasco.

d **Durante tu visita, vamos a** hacer muchas cosas. Vamos a visitar Bilbao. Y por supuesto el museo Guggenheim.

e Vamos a ir a la playa de Mundaka. ¡Va a ser superguay! **También quiero ir** a las fiestas de los pueblos.

f **Dime, ¿te gustaría** ir a un partido de fútbol del Athletic de Bilbao? El Athletic es el mejor equipo del mundo. Sus colores son el rojo y el blanco.
Tengo muchas ganas de conocerte. Bermeo te va a gustar mucho.

Hasta pronto,
Iñaki

ZONA CULTURA

El País Vasco

El País Vasco o Euskadi está situado en el norte de España.

En el País Vasco hay dos idiomas oficiales, el castellano y el euskera. El euskera es probablemente el idioma más antiguo de Europa.

leer 5 Lee el texto otra vez y completa las frases en inglés.

Ejemplo: **1** Iñaki lives with his mother, his stepfather and his sister.

1 Iñaki lives with …
2 Bermeo is in the Basque country, which …
3 Iñaki speaks …

4 During Liam's visit they are going to … (2 things)
5 Iñaki also wants to … (1 thing)
6 Iñaki asks Liam whether …

escribir 6 Escribe un correo al correspondiente que has elegido del ejercicio 1.
(Use the words highlighted in Iñaki's text to help you.)

escuchar 1 Escucha y lee.

1 Te presento a mi madre, Paula.

Mucho gusto.

2 Este es mi padrastro Aitor y esta es mi hermana Lorea.

Encantado.

3 ¿Qué tal el viaje?

Muy bien, gracias.

4 ¿Tienes hambre?

No, gracias. No tengo hambre, pero tengo sed.

¿Quieres agua, Coca-Cola …?

5 ¿Tienes sueño?

Sí, estoy un poco cansado …

¿Quieres ir a dormir?

¿**Tienes** hambre?	Are you hungry?
No **tengo** sed.	I'm not thirsty.
¿**Tienes** sueño?	Are you sleepy?

Masc. sing.	este	this (one)
Fem. sing.	esta	this (one)
Masc. plural	estos	these (ones)
Fem. plural	estas	these (ones)

hablar 2 Con tu compañero/a, haz un diálogo.

- Te presento …   ■ Mucho gusto.
-     ■ Encantado/Encantada.
- ¿viaje?   ■ ☺
- ¿ ?   ■ pero
- ¿Quieres un ? ¿Quieres ?   ■ Sí, quiero ✓

3 Escucha y escribe la letra correcta. (1–12)

Ejemplo: **1** d

 ¿Necesitas algo?

 Necesito …

a un cepillo de dientes

b una toalla

c jabón

d champú

e pasta de dientes

f un secador

¿Puedo …?

g escribir un correo a mis padres

h llamar a casa

i ver la tele

j ducharme

k cargar mi móvil

l acostarme

 4 Con tu compañero/a, haz diálogos.

- ● ¿Necesitas algo?
- ● ¿Necesitas … o …?
- ■ ¿Puedo …?

- ■ Necesito …, por favor.
- ■ No, gracias. Pero necesito …
- ● ¡Claro!

 5 Escucha y completa la canción. (1–7)

Ejemplo: **1** Coca-Cola

> *Bienvenido, bienvenido, mi casa es tu casa.*
> *Mira cómo lo vamos a pasar – ¡bomba, bomba, bomba!*
>
> *¿Qué tal el viaje? ¿Fue emocionante?*
> *¿Fue un poco aburrido o fue muy interesante?*
>
> *¿Tienes hambre, mi amigo? ¿Quieres comer algo?*
> *¿Quieres* **(1)** *o agua? ¿Qué hay en el frigorífico?*
>
> *¿Necesitas un cepillo o* **(2)** *?*
> *¿Jabón,* **(3)** *, un secador? ¿Necesitas* **(4)**  *?*
>
> *Este es tu* **(5)**  *, pero es un poco pequeño.*
> *¿Quieres dormir? ¿Quieres dormir? ¿Ya tienes sueño?*
>
> *¿Quieres cargar tu* **(6)** *o quieres ver la* **(7)** *?*
> *¿Necesitas algo más? ¿En qué puedo ayudarte?*
>
> *Bienvenido, bienvenido, mi casa es tu casa.*
> *Mira cómo lo vamos a pasar – ¡bomba, bomba, bomba!*

1 Escucha y escribe los destinos correctos. (1–8)

Ejemplo: **1** Oviedo

El tren con destino a … sale a …

| Oviedo | Burgos | Barcelona | Toledo |

| Vigo | Madrid | Valencia | Bilbao |

2 Escucha otra vez y escribe la letra correcta. (1–8)

1 a 12:10 b 02:10

2 a 14:40 b 14:48

3 a 17:32 b 17:36

4 a 18:22 b 18:24

5 a 16:50 b 16:54

6 a 20:04 b 20:02

7 a 21:16 b 21:17

8 a 19:23 b 19:25

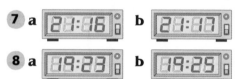

The 24-hour clock is used when talking about travel times.

13:21   las trece veintiuno
15:46   las quince cuarenta y seis
22:10   las veintidós diez

3 Escucha y lee. Luego copia y rellena la tabla.

No. of tickets	Single or return	Price	Departure time	Platform	Arrival time

- ● Buenos días.
- ■ Buenos días. ¿Qué quiere usted?
- ● Quiero dos billetes para Bilbao, por favor.
- ■ ¿Sólo de ida o de ida y vuelta?
- ● De ida y vuelta. ¿Cuánto es?
- ■ Son 12 euros.
- ● ¿A qué hora sale el tren?
- ■ Sale a las 9:48.
- ● ¿De qué andén sale?
- ■ Sale del andén 2.
- ● ¿Y a qué hora llega?
- ■ Llega a las 11:05.
- ● ¿Es directo?
- ■ Sí, es directo. No hay que cambiar.

billete = *ticket*

4 **Con tu compañero/a, haz estos diálogos.**

● Buenos días.
■ Buenos días. ¿Qué quiere usted?
● Quiero … por favor.
■ ¿Sólo de ida o de ida y vuelta?
● … ¿Cuánto es?
■ Son … euros.
● ¿A qué hora sale el tren?
■ Sale a las …
● ¿De qué andén sale?
■ Sale del andén …
● ¿Y a qué hora llega?
■ Llega a las …
● ¿Es directo?
■ Sí, es directo. No hay que cambiar.

A SAN SEBASTIÁN
1× ⟷
43 €
9:57 – 12:39
andén 3
✗

Usted is the formal singular 'you'. It uses the same verb form as 'he/she'.

¿Qué quiere **usted**?
What do you want?

B GERNIKA
3× →
20 €
11:48 – 12:15
andén 4
✔

C MUNDAKA
4× ⟷
6 €
14:12 – 15:24
andén 6
✔

 5 **Escucha y escribe la información que falta. (1–5)**

	CIUDAD	SALIDA	ANDÉN	LLEGADA	DIRECTO
1	Bilbao	8:18	? a	10:35	✗
2	? b	20:34	5	22:47	✔
3	Bérriz	11:18	6	13:50	? c
4	Durango	? d	3	10:12	✔
5	Eibar	20:43	1	? e	✔

BILBAO Bérriz
PAÍS VASCO
Eibar
Durango San Sebastián
Vitoria

 6 **Lee la información, luego lee las frases. ¿Verdadero (V) o falso (F)?**

Nº Tren	Tipo tren	Salida	Llegada	Período de circulación	Precio internet	
00201	TALGO	15:50	21:59	LMXJVD	Turista	38.20
					Turista Niño	22.90
					Preferente	50.60
					Preferente Niño	30.30

1 I can take the TALGO on a Saturday.
2 The TALGO arrives at 21:59.
3 The TALGO leaves at 22:45.
4 An adult tourist would pay 22.90€.

Mini-test

I can
● introduce myself to a penfriend
● say what I plan to do
● ask for things I need
● ask permission to do things
● buy a train ticket

4 Una excursión a Bilbao

 1 Escucha y escribe las letras correctas. (1–4)

Ejemplo: **1** g, …

¡Bienvenidos/as a Bilbao!

a
el museo Guggenheim

b
el puente Zubizuri

c
la catedral de Santiago

d
la plaza Moyúa

e
el teatro Arriaga

f
el palacio de Congresos y de la Música

g
el casco viejo

h
el museo de Bellas Artes de Bilbao

 2 Listen again and write down the phrases you hear with 'me/te gusta', 'no me gusta', 'me encanta'. Then translate the phrases into English.

Ejemplo: **1** me gusta la historia – *I like history*.

 3 Con tu compañero/a, haz diálogos.

● Me gusta <u>sacar fotos</u>.
■ Puedes visitar <u>el casco viejo</u>.

(No) Me gusta	el arte
	la historia
Me encanta	la música
	ir de compras
	ir al teatro
	sacar fotos
Puedes	visitar el/la …
	ir al/a la …

a
b
c
d
e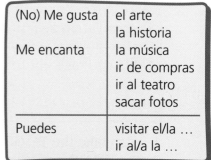
f

4 Escucha y lee. Escribe las letras del ejercicio 1 en el orden correcto.

Ejemplo: g, …

Liam: Iñaki, mañana vamos a ir a Bilbao en tren con Katia y Leyre, ¿no? Leyre es muy guapa, me gusta mucho. ¿Qué vamos a visitar?

Iñaki: Vamos a visitar el casco viejo. Hay muchas tiendas y comercios. A Katia le gusta ir de compras. Luego vamos ir a un bar a comer un pincho o dos.

Liam: Leyre va a comprar ropa también. A ella le gusta mucho ir de compras. Me gusta sacar fotos. Voy a sacar una foto a Leyre en la catedral de Santiago. ¿Vamos a visitar el teatro Arriaga?

Iñaki: Claro. Y también puedes sacar una foto de la plaza Moyúa. Es muy bonita. Luego vamos a visitar el museo Guggenheim. Es un museo muy famoso de arte contemporáneo.

Liam: ¡Genial!

Iñaki: Otro edificio que vamos a visitar es el palacio de Congresos y de la Música. Es muy moderno.

Liam: Y vamos a cruzar el puente Zubizuri. ¡Es muy famoso!

Iñaki: Hoy me voy a acostar pronto. ¡Mañana va a ser un día muy intenso!

¿no? = *aren't we?*
un pincho = *a small portion, snack*

To add emphasis, you can add in:

A mí, me gusta …   *I* like …
A ti, te gusta …   *You* like …
A Leyre le gusta …   *Leyre* likes …

5 Busca estos verbos en español en el texto y escríbelos en la columna correcta.

Present tense	Near future tense
	1 *vamos a ir*

1 we are going to go
2 we are going to visit
3 she likes to go shopping
4 she is going to buy
5 I like to take photos
6 I am going to take a photo
7 you can take a photo
8 we are going to cross
9 Tomorrow is going to be

6 Copia y completa el texto con palabras del cuadro.

Mañana **(1)** *vamos* a ir a Bilbao y vamos a **(2)** _____ muchas cosas interesantes. Me gusta mucho la arquitectura, por eso vamos **(3)** _____ visitar el palacio de Congresos y de la Música. Luego vamos a visitar el **(4)** _____. Me encanta el arte contemporáneo. Después vamos a **(5)** _____ un pincho en un bar. Vamos a **(6)** _____ muchas fotos. Yo voy a sacar fotos de edificios y de la gente.

Remember, the near future is formed using the present tense of **ir** and the **infinitive**.

voy a **sacar**   *I am going to take*
vas a **comprar**   *you are going to buy*
va a **visitar**   *he/she is going to visit*
vamos a **ir**   *we are going to go*

sacar	hacer	comer
museo Guggenheim	~~vamos~~	a

● Writing a letter
● Using the preterite and near future tenses together

 1 Escucha. Copia y rellena la tabla.

Ayer	i, …
Mañana	

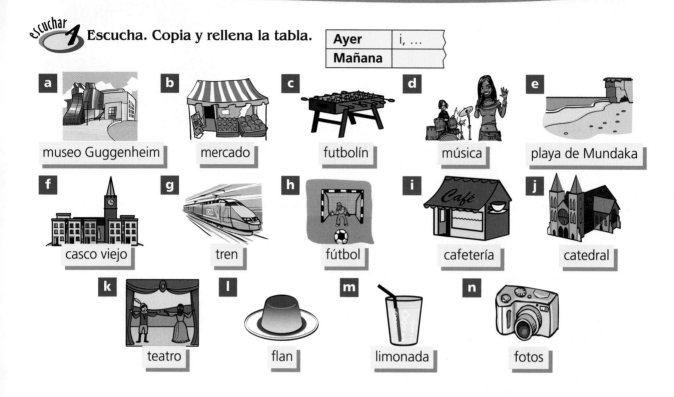

a museo Guggenheim
b mercado
c futbolín
d música
e playa de Mundaka
f casco viejo
g tren
h fútbol
i cafetería
j catedral
k teatro
l flan
m limonada
n fotos

2 Escucha otra vez y completa las frases en español. Luego traduce las frases al inglés.

Ejemplo: **1** En la cafetería comí un flan y jugué al futbolín. – *In the café I ate flan and played table football.*

1 En la cafetería ⁓⁓⁓ y ⁓⁓⁓.

2 Luego fuimos ⁓⁓⁓.

3 Vi ⁓⁓⁓.

4 Más tarde fuimos ⁓⁓⁓.

5 Pero yo ⁓⁓⁓.

6 Mañana vamos a ir ⁓⁓⁓.

7 Liam va a ⁓⁓⁓.

8 Yo voy a ⁓⁓⁓.

Gramática

ir, hacer and ver

These are important irregular verbs. Make sure you know them in these tenses.

	Preterite	Near future
ir *(to go)*		
I	fui	voy a ir
you	fuiste	vas a ir
he/she	fue	va a ir
we	fuimos	vamos a ir
hacer *(to do, to make)*		
I	hice	voy a hacer
you	hiciste	vas a hacer
he/she	hizo	va a hacer
we	hicimos	vamos a hacer
ver *(to see, to watch)*		
I	vi	voy a ver
you	viste	vas a ver
he/she	vio	va a ver
we	vimos	vamos a ver

Para saber más   página 000

3 Con tu compañero/a, haz diálogos.

● ¿Qué hiciste ayer en Bilbao?
■ Primero fui al/a la …y … Luego fui al/a al … y … Lo pasé …

● ¿Qué vas a hacer mañana?
■ Primero voy a ir al/a la … Voy a ir … Más tarde voy a … voy a jugar …

leer
4 Lee la carta. Luego lee las frases. ¿Verdadero (V) o falso (F)?

Ejemplo: **1** F

1 Iñaki fue a Bilbao con Liam, Katia y Lily.
2 A Iñaki no le gusta hacer turismo porque es aburrido.
3 Iñaki fue al museo Guggenheim pero no fue a la cafetería.
4 Mañana van a ir a la playa de Mundaka.
5 Iñaki va a nadar en el agua porque está caliente.

Bermeo, 5 de mayo

¡Querida Lily!

nadar = *to swim*

¿Cómo estás? Ayer fui a Bilbao con tu hermano Liam y dos chicas, Katia y Leyre. Fuimos en tren porque es muy rápido y además es muy cómodo.

Fuimos al casco viejo. Normalmente no me gusta mucho hacer turismo porque es aburrido, pero con Liam y Katia fue muy divertido. Vi la catedral de Santiago y el teatro Arriaga.

Más tarde fuimos al museo Guggenheim pero yo no entré. Fui a una cafetería. Allí escuché música, comí un pincho y un bocadillo y bebí una Coca-Cola.

Mañana vamos a ir a la playa de Mundaka. El agua no está muy caliente, por eso no voy a nadar. Pero voy a hacer surf y también voy a jugar al fútbol.

Un abrazo desde Bilbao …

Iñaki

escribir
5 Escribe una carta desde Bilbao a un(a) amigo/a español(a).

Ayer fui … con …
Fuimos en …
Fui a …
Más tarde fui a …
Vi … saqué … jugué … escuché …
Mañana voy a …

Resumen

Unidad 1

I can

- give personal details about myself

  Soy creativa y habladora. Toco la guitarra.
  Me encantan las comedias.

- start and end a letter

  ¡Querido Liam! Hasta pronto

- suggest activities for a visit

  Durante tu visita, vamos a ir a la playa.
  ¿Te gustaría ir a un partido de fútbol?

Unidad 2

I can

- say what I need

  Necesito un cepillo de dientes y una toalla.

- ask permission to do something

  ¿Puedo escribir un correo a mis padres?
  ¿Puedo llamar a casa?

- introduce family members

  Te presento a mi padre y a mi madre.
  Esta es mi hermana.

- say 'pleased to meet you'

  Mucho gusto. Encantado/Encantada.

- say how the journey was

  El viaje fue interesante/aburrido/emocionante.

- G use expressions with **tener** to say I am hungry, thirsty, tired

  ¿Tienes hambre? No tengo sed. Tengo sueño.

Unidad 3

I can

- understand the 24-hour clock

  13:21 las trece veintiuno
  15:46 las quince cuarenta y seis

- buy a train ticket

  Quiero un billete de ida y vuelta para …

- ask when a train leaves and arrives

  ¿A qué hora sale el tren? ¿Y a qué hora llega?

- ask from which platform a train leaves

  ¿De qué andén sale?

- ask if the train is direct

  ¿Es directo?

Unidad 4

I can

- name some places to visit in Bilbao

  el museo Guggenheim, el puente Zubizuri,
    la catedral de Santiago

- G use present and near future tenses together

  Me gusta sacar fotos. Voy a sacar una foto a Leyre.

- G use **A mí** … for emphasis

  A mí me gusta sacar fotos.

Unidad 5

I can

- use the past and future tenses together

  Ayer fui al museo Guggenheim. Mañana vamos a
    ir a la playa de Mundaka.

- G use a range of time expressions

  Primero … Luego … Después …

- G use the preterite of irregular verbs

  Vi la catedral de Santiago. Fui al museo Guggenheim.

Prepárate

 1 Escucha. Copia y rellena la tabla. (1–5)

	Destino	Salida	Andén	Llegada	¿Directo?
1	Barcelona				

leer 2 Lee el texto y rellena los espacios en blanco con las palabras del cuadro.

Ayer fui a Vitoria. **(1)** Fuimos en tren. El viaje **(2)** ____ bastante interesante. **(3)** ____ música y mandé mensajes a mis amigos con el móvil. Vitoria es la capital del País Vasco y **(4)** ____ una ciudad muy bonita.

(5) ____ en un restaurante en el centro. ¡Qué rico! Después de comer, jugué a la pelota en la calle: es un deporte tradicional vasco.

Mañana **(6)** ____ el museo de Ciencias Naturales y luego vamos a ir al casco viejo. **(7)** ____ unas fotos muy buenas.

fuimos   es   voy a sacar   escuché   fue   vamos a visitar   comí

hablar 3 Con tu compañero/a, haz un diálogo.

- Te presento
- ▪
- Este es … y este es …
- ▪ Encantado/Encantada.
- ¿viaje?
- ▪
- ¿ ?
- ▪ pero
- ¿Quieres un ? ¿Quieres ?
- ▪ Sí, quiero

escribir 4 Escribe planes para una visita a San Sebastián. Utiliza estas ideas.

Mañana vamos a ir a San Sebastián

Primero voy a ir …

y voy a …

Después voy a

y voy a … y …

Me gusta

Voy a

ciento siete **107**

¡Extra!

1 Escucha y lee. Copia y rellena la ficha en inglés.

El País Vasco, o Euskadi, está situado en el norte de España.

Vitoria es la capital del País Vasco. Es una ciudad histórica y es bastante tranquila, pero Bilbao, donde está el famoso museo Guggenheim, es la ciudad más importante. Bilbao es el centro comercial e industrial del País Vasco. Otra ciudad importante con su atmósfera exclusiva es San Sebastián, que está en la costa.

En el País Vasco se hablan dos idiomas, el castellano y el euskera.

El paisaje es impresionante con sus montañas, sus ríos, y sus cascadas. Al norte está el océano Atlántico.

Es una región bastante rica con mucha industria. El turismo también es una industria muy importante. Viene mucha gente para hacer alpinismo, senderismo, o ciclismo o para montar a caballo.

cascada = *waterfall*
hacer alpinismo = *to go climbing*
hacer senderismo = *to go hiking*

Region	Basque Country
Situation	
Capital	
Other important cities	
Languages	
Landscape	
Activities	

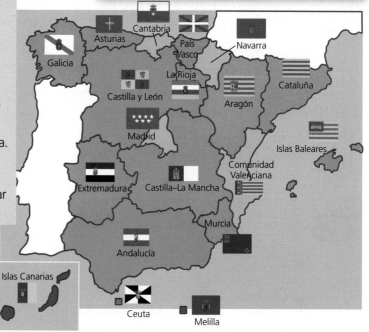

En España hay 19 comunidades autónomas.

2 Con tu compañero/a, pregunta y contesta sobre el País Vasco.

- ● ¿Cómo se llama esta región?
- ■ Se llama …
- ● ¿Dónde está?
- ■ Está en …
- ● ¿Cómo se llama la capital?
- ■ La capital se llama …
- ● ¿Hay otras ciudades importantes?
- ■ Otra ciudad importante es …
- ● ¿Qué idiomas hablan?
- ■ Hablan …
- ● ¿Cómo es el paisaje?
- ■ El paisaje es …
- ● ¿Qué se puede hacer en esta región?
- ■ En esta región se puede …

3 Escribe un párrafo sobre el País Vasco.

Esta región se llama …
Está en …
La capital se llama …
Otras ciudades importantes son …
El paisaje es …
En esta región se puede …

4 Lee el texto y termina las frases en inglés.

Ejemplo: **1** All year round, the temperatures in the Basque Country are mild.

---

www.paisvasco.net

El País Vasco

■ Clima

En el País Vasco, las temperaturas son suaves a lo largo de todo el año. Llueve más frecuentemente en la primavera y el otoño. En invierno no hace tanto frío y en verano no hace tanto calor. La temperatura media en verano es de 20°C y en invierno de 8°C.

■ Horarios de comidas

Las horas de comida habituales son:
Desayuno: de 8 a 10 horas.
Comida: de 13.30 a 15.30 horas.
Cena: de 21 a 23 horas.

■ Horarios laborales

Los horarios laborales más frecuentes en oficinas y despachos son:
Mañanas de 9 a 13 horas.
Tardes de 15 o 16 a 19 horas.
Los sábados la mayor parte de las oficinas están cerradas.

■ Idiomas

El País Vasco tiene dos idiomas oficiales: el euskera y el castellano. El castellano es hablado por la totalidad de los habitantes. El euskera es el idioma original del País Vasco.

---

1 All year round, the temperatures in the Basque Country are …
2 Rain is more frequent in …
3 The summers are not so …
4 In the morning, people work from … to …
5 In the afternoon, people work from … to …
6 Most offices are closed on …
7 Breakfast is normally from … to …
8 Lunch is normally from …to …
9 Dinner is normally from … to …
10 In the Basque Country, everyone speaks …

 5 Haz un póster sobre otra comunidad autónoma de España.

Choose another area of Spain that looks interesting.

- Find information from the internet to fill in the form in exercise 1.
- Then write a text (you can use the support from exercise 3 in order to do this).
- Try to add your opinion on why you would visit the region.

Me gustaría visitar esta región …

	es muy interesante
porque	el paisaje es impresionante
	se puede (+ *infinitive*)

Gramática

escribir 1 Write out the sentences correctly, then translate them into English.

Example: 1 ¿Tienes hambre? *Are you hungry?*

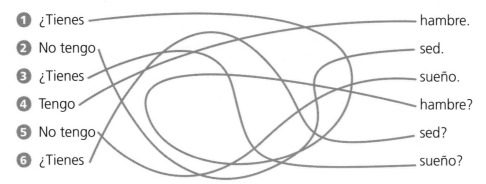

1. ¿Tienes — hambre.
2. No tengo — sed.
3. ¿Tienes — sueño.
4. Tengo — hambre?
5. No tengo — sed?
6. ¿Tienes — sueño?

escribir 2 Complete the sentences with words from the box.

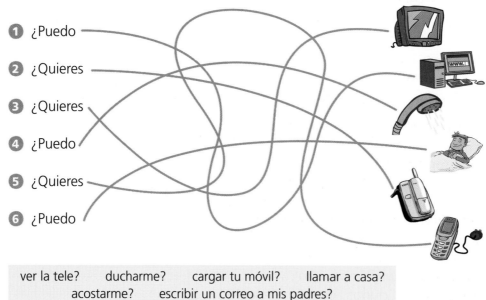

1. ¿Puedo
2. ¿Quieres
3. ¿Quieres
4. ¿Puedo
5. ¿Quieres
6. ¿Puedo

ver la tele?	ducharme?	cargar tu móvil?	llamar a casa?
acostarme?	escribir un correo a mis padres?		

escribir 3 Write logical sentences, using an element from each column.

Example: 1 Voy a ir a la playa porque me gusta nadar.

1. Voy a ir a la playa
2. Voy a ir al museo Guggenheim
3. Voy a ir al centro comercial
4. Voy a ir al casco viejo
5. Voy a ir a un restaurante
6. Voy a ir al concierto de jazz

porque

me gusta el arte.
me gusta la música.
me gusta ir de compras.
me gusta sacar fotos.
me gusta comer.
me gusta nadar.

escribir **4** Copy and complete the sentences with the correct form of **ir** and the correct infinitive. Use the pictures.

1 Vamos a ir al casco viejo. *(we)*

2 _____ al fútbol en la playa. *(he)*

3 _____ fotos a mi amigo Juan en la catedral. *(I)*

4 ¿_____ música? *(you, singular)*

5 _____ bocadillos en el mercado. *(they)*

6 _____ en la playa de Mundaka. *(you, plural)*

leer **5** Separate the preterite verbs in the wordsnake and complete the sentences.

1 – ¿_____ música ayer?
– Sí. _____ música de Enrique Iglesias.

2 – ¿_____ en coche al casco viejo?
– No. _____ a pie. Es más fácil.

3 – ¿Qué _____ durante tu visita?
– _____ muchas cosas interesantes.

4 – ¿_____ muchos monumentos en Bilbao?
– _____ el casco viejo y el puente Zubizuri.

5 – ¿_____ fotos de Bilbao?
– Sí. _____ muchas fotos. ¿Quieres verlas?

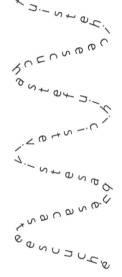

leer **6** Choose the correct answer to each question.

Example: 1 b

1 ¿Qué hiciste ayer?
  a Hago deporte.
  b Fui a Bilbao.
  c Voy a ir al teatro.
  d Me gusta jugar al tenis.

2 ¿Con quién fuiste?
  a Voy con mi abuela.
  b Voy a ir a un concierto.
  c Fui con mis amigas.
  d Fui en tren.

3 ¿Qué vas a hacer mañana?
  a Voy a ir al casco viejo a sacar fotos.
  b Saqué muchas fotos.
  c Vamos a pie.
  d Comí un bocadillo.

4 ¿Qué quieres hacer después?
  a Jugué al tenis.
  b Fui a un concierto.
  c Me gusta ir a la playa.
  d Quiero ir de compras.

5 ¿Qué te gusta hacer los domingos?
  a El domingo pasado fui a un concierto.
  b Los domingos me gusta ir al cine.
  c El domingo voy a ir a la playa.
  d Los fines de semana estudio.

Palabras

Me presento

Querido/a …
Tengo … años.
Vivo en … con …
Bermeo está en el
   País Vasco.
Es un pueblo en la
   costa.
Durante tu visita,
   vamos a …
También quiero ir a …
¿Te gustaría ir a …?

Tengo muchas ganas
   de conocerte.

Hasta pronto.

Te presento a …
Mucho gusto.
Este es mi padrastro.
Esta es mi hermana.
¿Qué tal el viaje?
Muy bien, gracias.
¿Tienes hambre/sed?
Tengo hambre.
Tengo sed.
¿Quieres agua?

¿Tienes sueño?
Estoy un poco
   cansado/a.
¿Quieres ir a dormir?

*Let me introduce
   myself*
Dear …
I'm … years old.
I live in … with …
*Bermeo is in the
   Basque Country.*
*It's a village on the
   coast.*
*During your visit,
   we're going to …*
I also want to go to …
*Would you like to go
   to …?*
*I'm really looking
   forward to meeting
   you.*
See you soon.

Let me introduce …
Pleased to meet you.
This is my stepfather.
This is my sister.
How was the journey?
Very good, thank you.
Are you hungry/thirsty?
I'm hungry.
I'm thirsty.
*Do you want some
   water?*
Are you sleepy?
I am a little tired.

*Do you want to go to
   bed?*

¿Necesitas algo?

Necesito …
un cepillo de dientes
champú
jabón
pasta de dientes
un secador
una toalla
¿Puedo …
   acostarme?
   cargar mi móvil?
   ducharme?
   escribir un correo
      a mis padres?
   llamar a casa?
   ver la tele?

En la estación
¿Qué quiere usted?
Quiero dos billetes
   para …, por favor.
¿Sólo de ida o de ida
   y vuelta?
¿Cuánto es?
Son … euros.
¿A qué hora sale el
   tren?
¿A qué hora llega el
   tren?
Sale a las …
Llega a las …
¿De qué andén sale?

Sale del andén …

¿Es directo?
(No) hay que cambiar.

*Do you need
   anything?*
I need …
a toothbrush
shampoo
soap
toothpaste
a hairdryer
a towel
Can I …
   go to bed?
   charge my mobile?
   have a shower?
   *send an email to
      my parents?*
   phone home?
   watch TV?

At the station
What do you want?
*I want two tickets
   to …, please.*
Single or return?

How much is it?
It is … euros.
*What time does the
   train leave?*
*What time does the
   train arrive?*
It leaves at …
It arrives at …
*Which platform does
   it leave from?*
*It leaves from
   platform …*
Is it direct?
*You (don't) have to
   change.*

Una excursión
Me gusta …
A mí me gusta …
A ti te gusta …
A Leyre le gusta …
ir de compras
ir al teatro
sacar fotos
el arte
la historia
la música
Puedes visitar …
el casco viejo
el museo de Bellas
    Artes de Bilbao
el museo
    Guggenheim
el palacio de
    Congresos y de
    la Música
el puente Zubizuri
el teatro Arriaga
la catedral de
    Santiago
la plaza Moyúa

An outing
I like …
I like …
You like …
Leyre likes …
going shopping
going to the theatre
taking photos
art
history
music
You can visit …
the old town
the Bilbao Fine Arts
    Museum
the Guggenheim
    Museum
the Palace of
    Congress and
    Music
the Zubizuri Bridge
the Arriaga Theatre
Santiago Cathedral

Moyúa Square

¿Qué hiciste?
¿Qué hiciste ayer en
    Bilbao?
Primero fui a la
    catedral.
Luego fui al museo
    Guggenheim.

Lo pasé fenomenal/
    bien.
¿Qué vas a hacer
    mañana?
Primero voy a ir al/a
    la …
Voy a sacar fotos.

Más tarde voy a ir
    de compras.

What did you do?
What did you do in
    Bilbao yesterday?
First I went to the
    cathedral.
Then I went to the
    Guggenheim
    Museum.
I had a fantastic/good
    time.
What are you going to
    do tomorrow?
First I'm going to go to
    the …
I'm going to take
    photos.
Later I'm going to go
    shopping.

Palabras muy útiles
primero
luego
después
porque
por eso

Very useful words
first of all
later
afterwards
because
so therefore

Estrategia

Revising your tenses

In order to get a high level, or to go on and get a good grade at GCSE it's really important to know your tenses. This module deals with past, present and future. To help you learn, start a list of verbs that you want to be able to use:

Infinitive (to …)	Present (I …)	Near future (I am going to …)	Past (I …)
ir	voy	voy a ir	fui

- Start with the verb forms you know and then try to work out the ones you're not sure of.

- Before you do a piece of writing involving different tenses, get your teacher to check what you have in the table to make sure it is all correct.

- Make a copy of the table and cut it up to test your classmates!

escribir 1 Unjumble the sentence starters and then cure the computer virus to complete the sentences logically.

Example: **1** Todos los días leo y escribo correos.

1 los y días leo Todos escribo …
2 cuando vez De descargo en …
3 tarde la navego Por …
4 semana de Los hago fines …
5 en De compro vez cuando …
6 la a veo Dos semana veces …
7 Nunca …
8 juego veces A …

```
1  c#rr##s
2  m#s#c#
3  p#r  #nt#rn#t
4  m#s  d#b#r#s
5  r#g#l#s
6  D##s
7  ch#t##
8  c#n  #l  #rd#n#d#r
```

 leer 2 Read the texts. True (T), false (F) or not mentioned (NM)?

Example: **1** F

1 Lola hates sports programmes.
2 Joaquín likes documentaries.
3 Joaquín thinks documentaries are informative.
4 Lola doesn't like the news.
5 Joaquín likes cartoons.
6 Lola thinks cartoons are stupid.
7 Joaquín likes the weather.
8 Lola thinks soaps are exciting.

> Me encantan los documentales porque son muy informativos y también son interesantes.
> Me gustan los dibujos animados porque son divertidos.
> No me gusta el programa del tiempo porque es aburrido. No es interesante.

> Me gustan mucho los programas de deporte. No son aburridos, son muy interesantes.
> Pero no me gustan nada las telenovelas. No son emocionantes. Son muy tontas.

Lola

Joaquín

escribir 3 Write out these sentences.

Example: **1** Las películas de terror son más aburridas que las películas de amor.

↑ = más … que
↓ = menos … que

1 ↑ aburridas  .

2 ↓ informativos .

3 ↓ divertidas .

4 ↓ interesantes .

5 ↑ tontas .

6 ↑ emocionantes .

leer 1 **Read the conversations. Copy the grid and fill it in.**

	Tipo de música	Opinión 👍 / 👎
Nuria	Música clásica	👍
Miguel		
Ana		
Javi		

1
● ¿Te gusta la música clásica, Nuria?
■ ¿La música clásica? Sí, me gusta bastante.

2
● ¿Te gusta la música electrónica, Miguel?
■ No, no me gusta nada la música electrónica.

3
● ¿Te gusta la música latina, Ana?
■ Ah sí, me encanta la música latina.

4
● ¿Te gusta el pop, Javi?
■ No. No me gusta el pop.
● ¿Y el jazz? ¿Te gusta el jazz?
■ Pues…, sí. Me gusta bastante.

 escribir 2 **Write out these conversations saying what you did last weekend.**

● ¿Qué hiciste el fin de semana pasado?
■ Fui a un concierto de Avril Lavigne.
　Fue fenomenal. Luego comí una pizza.

a concierto de Avril Lavigne

b concierto de 50 Cent

c concierto de Amy Winehouse

 leer 3 **Copy the text and fill in the gaps with the verbs from the box.**

Normalmente **(1)**juego con el ordenador todos los días. **(2)** ～ DVDs o
(3) ～ música y chateo un poco. Leo y **(4)** ～ correos todos los días.
También veo la televisión. Mi programa favorito es *La Isla de los Famosos*.
Es un programa de tele-realidad.

Me gusta el rock y ayer **(5)** ～ a un concierto de Marilyn Manson.
Fue genial. **(6)** ～ muchas fotos y **(7)** ～ una camiseta y unos CDs.
¡Qué guay! Después fui a un restaurante y **(8)** ～ una paella.

Esteban

| ~~juego~~ | veo | escribo | descargo | comí | saqué | fui | compré |

leer
1 *Write a summary of Ibrahim's school in English.*

Hola, me llamo Ibrahim. Vivo en Sevilla. Mi instituto se llama Instituto San Benito.

Es pequeño, hay quinientos alumnos y veinticinco profesores. Hay seis clases al día.

No llevo uniforme. No me gusta mucho mi instituto. Es un poco aburrido.

Name of school: San Benito school

Number of teachers:

Number of pupils:

Number of lessons:

Uniform:

Ibrahim's opinion:

escribir
2 *Write out the sentences in the wordsnakes correctly, then match them up to the correct set of pictures.*

Example: **1** Me gusta mucho el inglés porque es muy útil y es fácil. – **b**

1 Megustamuchoelinglésporqueesmuyútilyesfácil.

2 Megustalatecnologíaporqueesmuyinteresanteynoesdifícil.

3 Nomegustanadalahistoriaporqueesdifícil.

4 Nomegustannadalasmatemáticasporquesonaburridasydifíciles.

5 Megustamuchoelteatroporqueescreativoydivertido.

6 Nomegustamucholageografíaporquenoesinteresante.

escribir
3 *Write out the rules for this school.*

Example: No se debe llevar maquillaje.

Instituto Leyre

No se debe ...

Se debe ...

1 *True (T), false (F) or not mentioned (NM)?*

Example: **1** F

> Me llamo Letizia. Tengo catorce años. Mi instituto se llama Instituto Santa Cruz. Estudio inglés, matemáticas, español, ciencias y teatro. Me gusta mucho la informática y el año que viene voy a estudiar informática. También voy a estudiar comercio porque es interesante e importante. Me gusta mucho mi instituto. Hay muchas actividades. Los lunes voy al club de teatro después del colegio.

1 Letizia tiene quince años.
2 Estudia francés.
3 No le gustan las matemáticas.
4 Hay seis clases al día.
5 Va a estudiar comercio.
6 No le gusta mucho su instituto.

2 *Copy out the text and complete it with words from the box.*

El lunes **(1)** fui al club de fotografía en la hora de comer.

Después del colegio **(2)** ~~~ natación, luego **(3)** ~~~ al fútbol en el patio.

Ayer durante el recreo **(4)** ~~~ al club de informática. Más tarde, en la hora de comer, **(5)** ~~~ la guitarra en la orquesta y después del colegio **(6)** ~~~ en el coro.

| toqué | ~~fui~~ | jugué | hice | fui | canté |

3 *Write out which clubs these pupils went to yesterday.*

Example: Ayer fui al club de teatro en la hora de comer …

1

en la hora de comer

2

durante el recreo

3

en la hora de comer

después del colegio

después del colegio

después del colegio

Yolanda

Enrique

Raquel

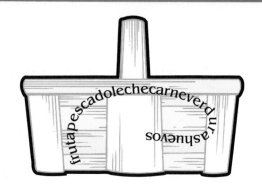

escribir 1 Separate out the food and drink words, then write a sentence about each one.

Example: La fruta es una comida sana.

sana	malsana

escribir 2 Find the right picture for each sentence and write out the sentences correctly. Then translate them into English.

Example: **1** Estoy enfermo. *I'm ill.*

1 Estoy *nf*rm*.

2 Tengo d**rr**.

3 Tengo t*s.

4 Tengo gr*p*.

5 Tengo c*t*rr*.

6 Tengo v*m*t*s.

7 Estoy c*ns*d*.

8 Tengo f**br*.

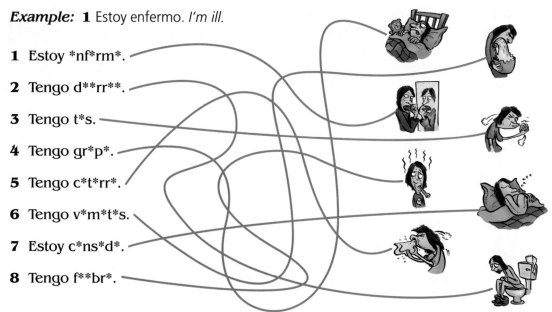

escribir 3 Crack the code, then write out the sentences and translate them into English.

Example: **1** Para llevar una vida más sana voy a hacer deporte.
To lead a more healthy life I am going to do sport.

1 Pluvmsvahd   **3** Pluvmsnvaccb   **5** Pluvmsvadohad
2 Pluvmsvaba   **4** Pluvmsnvaba   **6** Pluvmsnvatd

leer 4 Copy out and fill in the table in English.

Healthy food/drinks	Unhealthy food/drinks	Frequency
fruit		every day

Pues…, como fruta y verduras todos los días pero de vez en cuando como comida malsana, una hamburguesa por ejemplo, o pasteles. Pero nunca como patatas fritas. No me gustan nada. Bebo leche y agua todos los días, pero también bebo Coca-Cola de vez en cuando. Nunca bebo café porque es malsano.

1 Read the text, then complete the sentences in English.

Example: 1 The number of overweight children in Spain has tripled in the last fifteen years.

To help you understand the following text, you can use:
- your knowledge of healthy living
- cognates
- context
- common sense.

La obesidad en España

El número de niños obesos en España se ha triplicado en los últimos quince años. En este tiempo, el porcentaje ha pasado del 5% al 14%. Los niños comen comida basura en vez de fruta y verduras y tienen un estilo de vida más sedentario porque pasan muchas horas enfrente del ordenador.

Menos tele, más deporte

Hacer deporte frecuentemente es muy importante. Actualmente, la mayoría de los niños se pasan las tardes sentados frente al televisor o jugando con la videoconsola.

1 The number of overweight children in Spain has ⁓ in the last fifteen years.
2 It has risen from 5% to ⁓.
3 Children eat ⁓.
4 They don't eat enough ⁓ or ⁓.
5 ⁓ is very important.
6 Children spend too much time in front of the ⁓ or playing ⁓.

2 Copy out these conversations and fill in the gaps.

1 ● ¿Qué te duele?
■ Me duele *la pierna* y me duele también ⁓.

● ¿Desde hace cuánto tiempo?
■ Desde hace **4** días. Tengo ⁓ también.

● Tienes que tomar ⁓ y también

tienes que beber mucha ⁓.
■ Muy bien. Muchas gracias.

2 ● ¿Qué te duele?
■ Me duele ⁓ y me duele también ⁓.

● ¿Desde hace cuánto tiempo?
■ Desde hace **4** días. Tengo ⁓ también.

● Tienes que tomar ⁓ y también

tienes que beber mucha ⁓.
■ Muy bien. Muchas gracias.

3 ● ¿Qué te duele?
■ Me duele ⁓ y ⁓.

● ¿Desde hace cuánto tiempo?
■ Desde hace **3** días. Tengo ⁓ también.

● Tienes que tomar ⁓ y también tienes

que tomar ⁓.

leer 1 *Decode these jobs.*

Example: 1 profesora

1 ∩℘□‡†◆□℘<
2 Δ⊠Ω†⊠Δ†℘□
3 ‡★⊥=□πΔ◆⊥<
4 ℘†>†∩>Δ□⊠Δ◆⊥<
5 †⊠‡‡℘Ɣ†℘□
6 Ɣ§?Δ>□
7 ?Δ◆†Ο<?□℘<
8 >□>Δ⊠†℘□

<	a	Ɣ	m
=	b	⊠	n
>	c	Ο	ñ
?	d	□	o
†	e	∩	p
§	é	℘	r
‡	f	◆	s
Ω	g	⊥	t
Δ	i	★	u
π	l		

leer 2 *Cure the computer virus and write out the sentences correctly. Then translate them into English.*

1 MX gXstXríX trXbXjXr Xl XXrX lXbrX.
2 MX gXstXríX trXbXjXr cXn nXñXs.
3 MX gXstXríX trXbXjXr cXn XnXmXlXs.
4 MX gXstXríX trXbXjXr Xn XnX XfXcXnX.
5 MX gXstXríX trXbXjXr sXlX.
6 MX gXstXríX vXXjXr.
7 MX gXstXríX hXcXr Xn trXbXjX crXXtXvX.
8 MX gXstXríX trXbXjXr cXn gXntX.
9 MX gXstXríX hXcXr Xn trXbXjX mXnXXl.

escribir 3 *Write out these sentences in the present tense.*

Example: 1 Lavo el coche y hago de canguro. Con el dinero que gano, compro revistas, CDs y DVDs.

1 Copy out the text and fill the gaps with words from the box.

Me llamo Tania y **(1)**soy diseñadora. **(2)**_____ en una tienda de ropa. Me encanta mi trabajo. Soy paciente pero soy **(3)**_____. Creo que soy bastante práctica. Soy creativa **(4)**_____. El año pasado **(5)**_____ a Inglaterra para trabajar.

Fui a Newcastle para un proyecto. **(6)**_____ mucho. Lo pasé guay.

| me gustó | _soy_ | trabajo | fui | también | habladora |

 2 Read the text and answer the questions in English.

El año pasado trabajé en una cafetería en Barcelona como camarero. Puse las mesas, lavé los platos y limpié un poco después de la cena. Me gustó el trabajo pero no gané mucho dinero.

Este año trabajo en un restaurante en Barcelona y me gusta mucho porque hay mucha gente. Me gusta mucho trabajar con gente. No me gustaría nada trabajar solo.

Hablo inglés y español. El año que viene voy a estudiar francés. Quiero ir a Francia. Me encantaría trabajar en una cafetería en París.

1 What did Fernando do last year?
2 What exactly were his duties?
3 Where is he working this year?
4 Which languages does he speak?
5 What is he going to do next year?
6 Where would he love to work?

 3 Write a paragraph about these plans, using the exercise 2 text as a model.

El año pasado ——— Madrid

Este año ———

Barcelona

El año que viene ———.

Me gustaría trabajar ——— Londres.

leer 1 Write out the sentences correctly. Then match them up with the correct pictures.

Example: **1** Se debe comprar productos verdes. – **e**

1 Sedebecomprarproductosverdes.
2 Sedebereciclarpapelyvidrio.
3 Sedebereducirlacontaminación.
4 Sedebeusarmáseltransportepúblico.
5 Sedebeapagarlaluz.
6 Nosedebetirarbasuraalsuelo.

leer 2 Read the text, then answer the questions in English.

Example: **1** Colombia

Me llamo Gabriel García Márquez.
Soy de Colombia.
Nací el 6 de marzo de 1927 en Aracataca.
En 1982 gané el Premio Nobel de Literatura.
Me gustan los libros.

1 Where is Gabriel García Márquez from?
2 What is his date of birth?
3 Where exactly was he born?
4 What happened in 1982?
5 What does he like?

escribir 3 Write a text as if you were Gabriel Batistuta. Use the verbs underlined in exercise 2 to help you.

- Gabriel Batistuta
- Argentina
- 1 de febrero de 1969
- Avellaneda
- 1999 – el premio al mejor
  futbolista del año
- el fútbol y la televisión

escribir

1 Copy out the text and fill in the gaps with the words below.

Ejemplo: **1** Venezuela

Este país se llama **(1)**___. Está en Sudamérica. Está en **(2)**___. La capital de Venezuela se llama **(3)**___. La geografía es interesante. Hay **(4)**___, **(5)**___, **(6)**___, y **(7)**___. Los productos principales son **(8)**___, **(9)**___, **(10)**___.

montañas	la fruta	una llanura	la costa	el maíz
Caracas	el petróleo	Venezuela	ríos	selva

leer

2 Read the conversation, then put the topics into the order of the text.

María: Carlos, ¿adónde fuiste de vacaciones el año pasado?

Carlos: Pues… estuve en Argentina y en Chile y lo pasé genial. Me encanta Sudamérica. El año que viene quiero ir a Centroamérica: a Panamá o a Costa Rica. ¡Uf! Hay tanto que ver en Latinoamérica…

María: ¿Sí? ¿Y qué se puede hacer en Latinoamérica?

Carlos: Bueno, Latinoamérica es muy grande y hay una gran diversidad geográfica. Hay desiertos, montañas, volcanes y selvas. También hay una flora y fauna muy variada.

María: ¡Qué interesante! ¿Y cuáles son los principales productos de Latinoamérica?

Carlos: El café y el cacao son los productos más importantes, pero también el maíz, el tabaco y la caña de azúcar vienen de allí…

María: ¿Ah, sí? ¿Y se habla español?

Carlos: ¡Claro que sí! Aunque también se hablan dialectos indígenas como el quechua, el guaraní, …

María: ¿Y hay muchos turistas?

Carlos: Sí, hay muchos. En Latinoamérica hay playas preciosas y las puestas de sol son impresionantes.

María: Me encantaría viajar más, Carlos.

Carlos: A mí también, María… A mí también…

los animales

los productos

el turismo

la geografía

los idiomas

todavía = *still*

leer

3 Read the conversation again. Decide whether these statements are true (T), false (F) or not mentioned (NM).

Example: **1** F

1 Carlos fue a México.
2 A María le gustó Argentina.
3 En Sudamérica se habla español.

4 Es muy caro hacer turismo en Sudamérica.
5 Muchos turistas visitan Argentina, Perú y Chile.
6 A María no le gustaría viajar.

Te toca a ti A

escribir 1 *Write out these conversations.*

Example: – ¿Necesitas algo?
– A ver… necesito un cepillo de dientes y pasta de dientes… y ¿puedo llamar a casa?

leer 2 *Read the letter and answer the questions in English.*

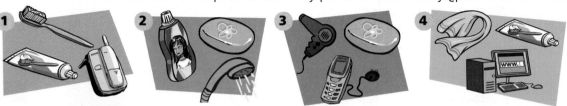

Whitley Bay, 15 de julio

Querida Lola,

Me presento. Soy Mandy. Tengo catorce años. Vivo en Whitley Bay con mi madre, mi padre, mi hermana y mis dos perros. Whitley Bay está en el norte de Inglaterra.

Hablo inglés y estudio español y francés en el instituto.

Durante tu visita, vamos a hacer muchas cosas. Newcastle tiene muchos monumentos interesantes. Hay museos y un castillo y se puede ir de compras también.

Vamos a ir al cine y a la playa. En la playa podemos hacer surf. También vamos a ver un partido de fútbol de Newcastle United, el mejor equipo del mundo.

¡Tengo muchas ganas de conocerte!
Hasta pronto,

Mandy

1 How old is Mandy?
2 Who does Mandy live with?
3 Where is Whitley Bay?
4 Which languages is Mandy studying?
5 What is there to do in Newcastle?
6 What are they going to do during Lola's visit?
7 What can you do on the beach?
8 What does Mandy say about Newcastle United?

escribir 3 *Write a letter to a penfriend, using Mandy's letter as a model. Start and end your letter properly. Use the details below and add any others you wish.*

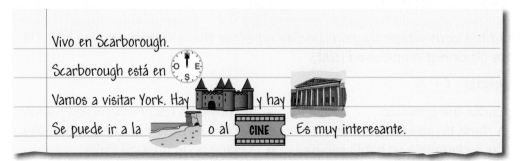

Vivo en Scarborough.
Scarborough está en
Vamos a visitar York. Hay   y hay
Se puede ir a la   o al CINE. Es muy interesante.

Copy and complete the dialogue using phrases from the box.

- ● Te presento a mi madre.
- ■ Mucho gusto.
- ● Este es mi padre y estas son mis hermanas, Anita y Carolina.
- ● ¿Qué tal el viaje?
- ■ …
- ● ¡Qué pena!
- ● …
- ■ No, gracias, no tengo hambre.
- ● …
- ■ No, gracias, no tengo sed.
- ● …
- ■ Sí, estoy un poco cansada …
- ● …

> ~~Mucho gusto.~~
> ¿Quieres ir a dormir?
> ¿Tienes sed?
> Fue un poco aburrido.
> ¿Tienes hambre?
> ¿Tienes sueño?

 Write out the times correctly. Then match each one with the correct clock.

1 Sonlascatorcediez.

5 Sonlasveintitréscincuenta.

2 Sonlasveintecuarentayocho.

6 Sonlasveintidóscerocinco.

3 Sonlasdiecisietetreintaynueve.

7 Sonlasveintiunadieciocho.

4 Sonlasdiecinueveveinticuatro.

8 Sonlasdieciochoveinticinco.

a 20:48 b 22:05 c 04:10 d 18:26 e 17:39 f 23:50 g 20:48 h 19:24

Write out these conversations. Change the underlined words.

- ● Buenos días.
- ■ Buenos días. ¿Qué quiere usted?
- ● Quiero <u>dos billetes para Madrid</u>, por favor.
- ■ ¿Sólo de ida o de ida y vuelta?
- ● <u>De ida y vuelta</u>. ¿Cuánto es?
- ■ Son <u>42</u> euros.
- ● ¿A qué hora sale el tren?
- ■ Sale a las <u>9:17</u>.
- ● ¿De qué andén sale?
- ■ Sale del andén <u>2</u>.
- ● ¿Y a qué hora llega?
- ■ Llega a las <u>13:05</u>.
- ● ¿Es directo?
- ■ Sí, es directo. No hay que cambiar.

A BARCELONA
3× →
60 €
14:38
andén 5
16:15

B VALENCIA
4× ↔
88 €
17:32
andén 8
19:14

Gramática

1   Nouns

A noun is a word that names a person or thing. In Spanish all nouns have a **gender**: masculine or feminine.

- Nouns ending in **-o** are usually masculine (e.g. **estómago**)
- Nouns ending in **-a** are usually feminine (e.g. **cabeza**)
- For other nouns, you need to learn the gender when you learn the word: **el café** (masculine), **la leche** (feminine).

How nouns change in the plural:

ends in a vowel	add **-s**	libro**s** *books*
ends in a consonant	add **-es**	móvil**es** *mobile phones*
ends in **-z**	change **z** to **c** and add **-es**	lápi**zces** *pencils*

2   Articles

In Spanish, words for 'a' and 'some' and 'the' change depending on whether the noun is masculine, feminine, singular or plural.

	Indefinite article	
	a	**some**
masculine	**un** libro	**unos** libros
feminine	**una** mochila	**unas** mochilas

	Definite article	
	the	**the (plural)**
masculine	**el** ordenador	**los** ordenadores
feminine	**la** ventana	**las** ventanas

3   Pronouns

Spanish has words for 'I', 'you', 'he', 'she', etc., but generally they are not used with verbs: the verb on its own is enough. However, you do need to be able to recognise them.

yo	*I*
tú	*you (singular)*
él	*he*
ella	*she*
nosotros/as	*we (male/female)*
vosotros/as	*you (plural, male/female)*
ellos/as	*they (male/female)*

4   Adjectives

Adjectives are words that describe nouns, e.g. a **big** elephant.

Adjectives you have met already in this course are words like **divertido**, **grande**, **interesante**. In Spanish the endings of adjectives change to match the noun they describe.

ending in ...	Singular		Plural	
	masc.	fem.	masc.	fem.
-o or -a	divertido	divertida	divertidos	divertidas
-e	grande	grande	grandes	grandes
-or	hablador	habladora	habladores	habladoras
other consonant	fácil	fácil	fáciles	fáciles

Most adjectives **follow** the noun they describe:

Tiene los ojos **marrones**.   *She has **brown** eyes.*

5   Colours and nationalities

Colour words are adjectives and follow the patterns shown above.

A few are irregular, changing only in the plural, e.g.

rosa – rosas *(pink)* and naranja – naranjas *(orange)*.

Nationalities are also adjectives, but those ending in a consonant follow a different pattern from the one shown above.

ending in ...	Singular	
	masculine	feminine
-o or -a	mexicano	mexicana
-e	estadounidense	estadounidense
consonant	escocés	escocesa

ending in ...	Plural	
	masculine	feminine
-o or -a	mexicanos	mexicanas
-e	estadounidenses	estadounidenses
consonant	escoceses	escocesas

6   Comparing things

When you want to compare two things, you use the comparative form of the adjective:

más + adjective + **que** = *more … than*
menos + adjective + **que** = *less … than*

The adjective agrees with the noun it describes.

Las comedias son **más divertidas que** las películas de amor.
*Comedies are **funnier** (literally: **more funny**) **than** romantic films.*

Los dibujos animados son **menos interesantes que** las películas de guerra.
*Cartoons are **less interesting than** war films.*

Superlatives

When you want to say 'the biggest', 'the smallest', etc., you use the superlative form of the adjective. It consists of the appropriate definite article + **más/menos** + adjective. The adjective agrees with the noun it describes.

Este vestido es **el más cómodo**.
*This dress is **the most comfortable**.*
Estas botas son **las menos prácticas**.
*These boots are **the least practical**.*

7   My, your, his, her

Words in Spanish for 'my', 'your', 'his', 'her' are called possessive adjectives. They agree with the noun they describe.

	Singular	Plural
my	mi hermano/a	mis hermanos/as
your	tu hermano/a	tus hermanos/as
his/her/its	su hermano/a	sus hermanos/as

8   Regular verbs (present tense)

The present tense is used to talk about what usually happens, e.g. I **go** to school every day.

It is also used to say what things are like, e.g. French lessons **are** very boring.

In Spanish it can also be used to talk about what is happening now, e.g. I **am doing** my homework.

These are the endings for regular **-ar** verbs in Spanish

Gramática

	-ar verbs
	hablar – *to speak*
(yo – *I*)	habl**o**
(tú – *you*)	habl**as**
(él/ella – *he/she*)	habl**a**
(nosotros/as – *we*)	habl**amos**
(vosotros/as – *you*)	habl**áis**
(ellos/as – *they*)	habl**an**

These are the endings for regular **-er** and **-ir** verbs in Spanish

	-er verbs	-ir verbs
	comer – *to eat*	**escribir** – *to write*
(yo – *I*)	com**o**	escrib**o**
(tú – *you*)	com**es**	escrib**es**
(él/ella – *he/she*)	com**e**	escrib**e**
(nosotros/as – *we*)	com**emos**	escrib**imos**
(vosotros/as – *you*)	com**éis**	escrib**ís**
(ellos/as – *they*)	com**en**	escrib**en**

9 Stem-changing verbs (present tense)

In the present tense, stem-changing verbs sometimes have a vowel change in the stem. The stem is the first part of the verb. They are usually regular in their endings.

	jugar – *to play*	**querer** – *to want*
(yo)	j**ue**go	qu**ie**ro
(tú)	j**ue**gas	qu**ie**res
(él/ella)	j**ue**ga	qu**ie**re
(nosotros/as)	jugamos	queremos
(vosotros/as)	jugáis	queréis
(ellos/as)	j**ue**gan	qu**ie**ren

Other examples of stem-changing verbs:

ac**o**starse *(to go to bed)* → me ac**ue**sto *(I go to bed)*
desp**e**rtarse *(to wake up)* → me desp**ie**rto *(I wake up)*
d**o**rmir *(to sleep)* → d**ue**rmo *(I sleep)*
p**o**der *(to be able to, can)* → p**ue**do *(I can)*

10 Irregular verbs (present tense)

Some verbs are not regular in the present tense: they don't follow the usual patterns for **-ar**, **-er** or **-ir** verbs.

Here are some verbs that are irregular in the 'I' form (the first person):

hacer *(to make/do)*   **hago**
poner *(to put)*   **pongo**
salir *(to go out)*   **salgo**
tener *(to have)*   **tengo***
ver *(to see)*   **veo**

***Tener** is also stem-changing: **tienes**, etc.

11 Reflexive verbs (present tense)

Reflexive verbs describe an action which you do to yourself. To show this, they include a pronoun which means 'myself', 'yourself', etc.

	ducharse – *to shower*	**despertarse** – *to wake up* (stem-changing)
(yo)	**me** ducho	**me** desp**ie**rto
(tú)	**te** duchas	**te** desp**ie**rtas
(él/ella)	**se** ducha	**se** desp**ie**rta
(nosotros/as)	**nos** duchamos	**nos** despertamos
(vosotros/as)	**os** ducháis	**os** despertáis
(ellos/as)	**se** duchan	**se** desp**ie**rtan

When you translate the verbs into English, you sometimes drop the pronoun. For example, instead of saying 'I shower myself', you just say 'I shower'.

12 *ser* and *estar*

In Spanish there are two verbs meaning *to be*: **ser** and **estar**.

Ser is used to refer to ongoing or permanent states:

Soy alto.	*I'm tall.*
El perro **es** negro.	*The dog is black.*
¿Cómo **eres**?	*What are you like?*

It is also used for telling the time:

¿Qué hora **es**?   *What time is it?*
Son las cuatro.   *It's 4 o'clock.*

Estar is used to refer to position and temporary conditions:

¿Dónde **está**?   *Where is it?*
¿Cómo **estás**?   *How are you?*
Estoy bien.   *I'm fine.*

13 The preterite: -ar verbs

The preterite or 'simple past tense' is used to talk about events in the past that are now finished.

When forming the preterite tense of regular **-ar** verbs, take off the **-ar** and add these endings:

	-ar verbs	
	visita**r** – *to visit*	
(yo)	visit**é**	*I visited*
(tú)	visit**aste**	*you visited (singular)*
(él/ella)	visit**ó**	*he/she visited*
(nosotros/as)	visit**amos**	*we visited*
(vosotros/as)	visit**asteis**	*you visited (plural)*
(ellos/as)	visit**aron**	*they visited*

A few **-ar** verbs have a spelling change in the 'I' form (the first person) before the **é** ending:

jugar → jug**u**é, navegar → naveg**u**é,
sacar → sa**qu**é

This is so that the 'g' or 'k' sound in the infinitive stays the same when you add the **é**.

14 The preterite: -er and –ir verbs

The preterite or 'simple past tense' is used to talk about events in the past that are now finished.

When forming the preterite tense of regular **-er** and **-ir** verbs, take off the **-er** or **-ir** and add these endings:

	-er verbs	-ir verbs
	com**er** – *to eat*	sal**ir** – *to go out*
(yo)	com**í**	sal**í**
(tú)	com**iste**	sal**iste**
(él/ella)	com**ió**	sal**ió**
(nosotros/as)	com**imos**	sal**imos**
(vosotros/as)	com**isteis**	sal**isteis**
(ellos/as)	com**ieron**	sal**ieron**

15 The preterite: irregular verbs

The verbs **ir** *(to go)* and **ser** *(to be)* are irregular in the preterite. They share the same forms, but the context makes it clear which verb is meant.

	ir – *to go*	
(yo)	fui	*I went*
(tú)	fuiste	*you went (singular)*
(él/ella)	fue	*he/she went*
(nosotros/as)	fuimos	*we went*
(vosotros/as)	fuisteis	*you went (plural)*
(ellos/as)	fueron	*they went*

	ser – *to be*	
(yo)	fui	*I was*
(tú)	fuiste	*you were (singular)*
(él/ella)	fue	*he/she was*
(nosotros/as)	fuimos	*we were*
(vosotros/as)	fuisteis	*you were (plural)*
(ellos/as)	fueron	*they were*

16 The near future tense

The near future tense is used to talk about what you are *going to* do.

It is formed as follows: present tense of **ir** + **a** + a verb in the infinitive.

Mañana **voy a ir** al cine.
*Tomorrow I'm going **to go** to the cinema.*
Vamos a ver una comedia.
*We're going **to see** a comedy.*
¿Qué **vas a hacer**?
*What are you going **to do**?*

When you are using the near future tense, check that you are using the correct form of **ir**:

	ir – *to go*
(yo)	voy
(tú)	vas
(él/ella)	va
(nosotros/as)	vamos
(vosotros/as)	vais
(ellos/as)	van

} + infinitive

17 Negatives

To make a sentence or a question negative, put **no** before the verb.

No voy a ir al cine.
I'm not going to go to the cinema.
¿Qué **no** te gusta?
What don't you like?

nunca (never)
Nunca can be used on its own before the verb.

Nunca veo la tele.   *I never watch TV.*

It can also be used in the pattern **no** + verb + **nunca** + rest of sentence.

No veo **nunca** la tele.

nada (nothing, not at all)
Nada is used in the pattern **no** + verb + **nada** + rest of sentence.

No hago **nada**.
I don't do anything. (= I do nothing.)
No le gusta **nada** ir de compras.
He doesn't like going shopping at all.

18 Expressing opinions

Expressing opinions will help you to reach a higher level in your speaking and writing.

Here is a list of phrases that you can use to express yourself better:

me gusta *(I like)*
me encanta *(I love)*
me interesa *(I am interested in)*

prefiero *(I prefer)*
odio *(I hate)*

There are three things to remember about these expressions:

- If you are talking about something you like **doing**, they need to be followed by an **infinitive**, e.g. Me gusta **ir** al cine.
- If you are talking about an object or thing that you like, make sure you include a definite article, e.g. Me interesa **la** historia.
- If there is more than one thing, then you need to add an **-n** to me gusta, me encanta and me interesa, e.g. me interesa**n** los cómics.

19 Modals with the infinitive

Modal verbs are followed by an infinitive.

- querer *(to want)*
  Quiero ir a la discoteca.
  I want to go to the disco.

- poder *(to be able to, can)*
  Puedo hacer mis deberes.
  I can do my homework.

- deber *(to have to, must)*
  Debo ordenar mi dormitorio.
  I must tidy my bedroom.

20 Other structures with the infinitive

A range of other verbs and structures can be followed by an infinitive.

impersonal structures
- se debe *(you/one must)*
  Se debe **hacer** tus deberes.
  *You must **do** your homework.*

- hay que *(you/one must)*
  Hay que **hacer** tus deberes.
  *You must **do** your homework.*

the near future tense

- voy a *(I'm going to)*
  Voy a **ir** al cine.
  *I'm going **to go** to the cinema.*

tener que

- tengo que *(I have to)*
  Tengo que **hacer** mis deberes.
  *I have **to do** my homework.*

21 Time expressions and adverbs of frequency

To add more detail to your speaking and writing make sure you add:

- Time expressions (past to future)

el año   la semana   el fin de   anteayer   ayer
pasado   pasada   semana
                       pasado

mañana   pasado   la semana   el año que
             mañana   que viene   viene

- Frequency expressions (always to never)

nunca   de vez en   a   normalmente   a   siempre
        cuando   veces   menudo

22 Connectives

Try to use these phrases to make your sentences longer and give more detail.

y *(and)*
Hago natación **y** voy al cine.
*I go swimming **and** I go to the cinema.*

pero *(but)*
Hago natación **pero** no voy al cine.
*I go swimming **but** I don't go to the cinema.*

también *(also)*
Hago natación y **también** voy al cine.
*I go swimming and I **also** go to the cinema.*

normalmente *(normally)*
Normalmente hago natación y voy al cine.
***Normally** I go swimming and I go to the cinema.*

primero *(first of all)*
Primero hago natación.
***First of all** I go swimming.*

luego *(later on)*
Luego voy al cine.
***Later on** I go to the cinema.*

después *(after that)*
Después voy al cine.
***After that** I go to the cinema.*

23 Qualifiers

muy *very*	Es **muy** caro.	*It's **very** expensive.*
bastante *quite/fairly*	Es **bastante** caro.	*It's **fairly** expensive.*
un poco *a bit*	Es **un poco** caro.	*It's **a bit** expensive.*

24 Numbers

0	cero
1	uno
2	dos
3	tres
4	cuatro
5	cinco
6	seis
7	siete
8	ocho
9	nueve
10	diez
11	once
12	doce
13	trece
14	catorce
15	quince
16	dieciséis
17	diecisiete
18	dieciocho
19	diecinueve
20	veinte
21	veintiuno
22	veintidós
23	veintitrés
30	treinta
31	treinta y uno
32	treinta y dos

40	cuarenta
50	cincuenta
60	sesenta
70	setenta
80	ochenta
90	noventa
100	cien
200	doscientos
250	doscientos cincuenta
300	trescientos
400	cuatrocientos
500	quinientos
600	seiscientos
700	setecientos
800	ochocientos
900	novecientos
1000	mil
2000	dos mil
2753	dos mil setecientos cincuenta y tres

25 Days

lunes
martes
miércoles
jueves
viernes
sábado
domingo

26 Months

enero
febrero
marzo
abril
mayo
junio
julio
agosto
septiembre
octubre
noviembre
diciembre

27 The time

Es la una.
Son las dos. (etc.)

menos cinco — y cinco
menos diez — y diez
menos cuarto — y cuarto
menos veinte — y veinte
menos veinticinco — y veinticinco
y media

28 Colours

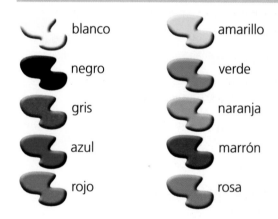

blanco	amarillo
negro	verde
gris	naranja
azul	marrón
rojo	rosa

29 Tips for getting level 5

Here is a checklist of things that will help you to reach level 5. When you are doing a piece of writing, use it to help you reach level 5.

★ Give opinions
★ Ask a question
★ Include more than one tense
★ Check your spellings of new or difficult words
★ Re-read your work to check your verbs and adjectives.

Give opinions and extra information

Say what you think of some things you mention.
Hago natación. → Hago natación. Me gusta mucho porque es divertido.

Fui de compras. → Fui de compras y lo pasé bomba. Compré muchas cosas …

Voy a ir a Francia. → Voy a ir a Francia. Va a ser estupendo porque voy ir a Disneyland Paris.

Ask a question

If you are speaking or writing a letter to someone, make sure you ask a question.

¿Te gusta …/Te gustan …?
¿Te gusta ir de compras?
¿Te gustan los caramelos?

Include more than one tense

Make sure you include information about the past or the future in your writing, as well as talking about the present:

Me gusta ir de compras. La semana pasada fui de compras y compré unos vaqueros y un jersey.

Me gusta ir de compras. La semana que viene voy a ir de compras. Voy a comprar unos vaqueros y un jersey.

Check the spellings of new or difficult words

Use the **Vocabulario** or use a dictionary to check you have chosen the right word and know how to spell it.

Re-read your work to check for mistakes

• Have you used infinitives after phrases like 'voy a …' and 'me gusta'?
• If using regular preterite verbs, have you remembered the accents: compré, comí, bebí?
• Have you used the correct endings on adjectives: divertido, divertida, divertidos, divertidas?
• Have you included the right punctuation? Remember in particular question marks and exclamation marks: ¿? ¡!

Vocabulario español–inglés

A

a *to*
a menudo *often*
¿a qué hora? *what time?*
abril *April*
aburrido/a *boring*
¡qué aburrido! *how boring!*
el accidente *accident*
la acción *action*
el aceite de oliva *olive oil*
acostarse *to go to bed, lie down*
activo/a *active*
el actor *actor*
la actriz *actress*
actualmente *today, at the moment*
actuar *to act*
acuático/a *underwater, aquatic*
me acuesto *I go to bed*
acusar *to accuse*
además *what's more*
adjuntar *to attach*
agosto *August*
el agricultor *farmer (m)*
la agricultora *farmer (f)*
el agua (f) *water*
ahora *now*
ahorrar *to save*
al aire libre *in the open air*
el ajedrez *chess*
alegre *lively*
el alemán *German (language)*
Alemania *Germany*
alguien *someone*
algún, alguno/a *some, a few*
el alpinismo *mountaineering*
alto/a *high*
la alumna *pupil (f)*
el alumno *pupil (m)*
la amiga *friend (f)*
el amigo *friend (m)*
el amor *love*
el andén *platform*
el año escolar *school year*
el Año Nuevo *New Year*
el año pasado *last year*
el año que viene *next year*
anteayer *the day before yesterday*
antiguo/a *old, ancient*
antipático/a *unpleasant, nasty*
apagar *to switch off*
aparecer *to appear*
el apellido *surname*
no me apetece *I don't fancy it*
aprender *to learn*
el árbol de Navidad *Christmas tree*
el arroz *rice*
el arte *art*
las artes marciales *martial arts*
asado/a *roast*
la asignatura *subject*
la aspiradora *vacuum cleaner*
la aspirina *aspirin*

auténtico/a *authentic, real*
la aventura *adventure*
el avión *plane*
ayer *yesterday*
ayudar *to help*
el azúcar *sugar*

B

bailar *to dance*
la bailarina *dancer (f)*
el baile *dance*
bajo/a *low, short*
el baloncesto *basketball*
el barrio *suburb, district*
básico/a *basic*
bastante *enough, quite*
la basura *rubbish, litter*
beber *to drink*
bebí *I drank*
la bebida *drink*
bebo *I drink*
el belén *crib, Nativity scene*
la biblioteca *library*
bien *well, fine*
¡qué bien! *great!*
bienvenido/a *welcome*
bilingüe *bilingual*
el billete *ticket*
el billete de ida *single ticket*
el billete de ida y vuelta *return ticket*
blanco/a *white*
la boca *mouth*
el bocadillo *sandwich*
bomba *fantastic*
bonito/a *nice*
la botella *bottle*
el brazo *arm*
bueno/a *good*
buscar *to search/look for*

C

el caballo *horse*
la cabeza *head*
el cacao *cocoa*
cada *each, every*
el café *coffee*
me caí *I fell*
la calidad *quality*
caliente *warm*
la calle *street*
la cama *bed*
la camarera *waitress*
el camarero *waiter*
cambiar *to change*
caminar *to walk*
el camión *bus (L Am), lorry (Sp)*
la camiseta *T-shirt*
la caña de azúcar *sugar cane*
cansado/a *tired*
el cantante *singer (m)*
la cantante *singer (f)*
cantar *to sing*
la cantina *canteen, dining hall*

la cara *face*
el caramelo *sweet*
el carbón *coal*
cargar *to charge (up)*
el Caribe *Caribbean*
la carne *meat*
el carro *car (L Am)*
la casa *house*
la cascada *waterfall*
el casco viejo *old town*
casi *almost*
el castellano *Castilian (Spanish)*
el castillo *castle*
el catalán *Catalan (language)*
el catarro *cold*
la catedral *cathedral*
cenar *to have dinner*
el centro *centre*
el cepillo de dientes *toothbrush*
cerrado/a *closed*
la chabola *shack, hovel*
el champán *champagne*
el champú *shampoo*
chatear *to chat online*
la chica *girl*
el chicle *chewing gum*
el chico *boy*
la ciencia-ficción *sci-fi*
las ciencias *science(s)*
el cigarrillo *cigarette*
el cine *cinema*
la ciudad *city*
¡claro que sí! *of course!*
la clase *lesson*
clásico/a *classical*
el clima *climate*
el club de teatro *drama club*
el coche *car*
la cocina *kitchen*
la cocinera *cook, chef (f)*
el cocinero *cook, chef (m)*
coger *to catch*
la comedia *comedy*
comer *to eat*
el comerciante *businessman*
la comerciante *businesswoman*
el comercio *business studies, trade*
el comercio justo *fair trade*
comí *I ate*
la comida *food*
la comida basura *junk food*
la comida rápida *fast food*
la comisaría *police station*
¿cómo? *what?, how?*
cómodo/a *comfortable*
comprar *to buy*
compré *I bought*
compro *I buy*
las comunidades autónomas *autonomous regions (of Spain)*
con *with*
el concierto *concert*
el concurso *game show*
conducir *to drive*
el conductor *driver (m)*
la conductora *driver (f)*

conduzco *I drive*
el conejo *rabbit*
conocer *to know (a person or place)*
la contaminación *pollution*
el coro *choir*
corregir *to correct*
correr *to run*
la cosa *thing*
la costa *coast*
creativo/a *creative*
el crédito *credit*
cruzar *to cross*
¿cuál(es)? *which?, what?*
cuando *when*
¿cuándo? *when?*
¿cuánto/a? *how much?, how many?*
el cuerpo *body*
¡cuidado! *be careful!*
cultivar *to cultivate, grow*
la cultura *culture*

D

da igual *it doesn't matter*
los datos *details*
se debe *you must*
deber *to have to, must*
los deberes *homework*
debería *he/she/one should*
debes *you must*
debo *I must*
decir *to say*
decorar *to decorate*
el dedo *finger*
dejar *to leave*
demasiado *too much*
demasiado/a *too*
el deporte *sport*
la derecha *right*
desafinar *to sing out of tune*
desaparecer *to disappear*
desarrollado/a *developed*
el desarrollo *development*
desayunar *to have breakfast*
descargar *to download*
descargué *I downloaded*
la descripción *description*
desde *since*
desde hace *for (time)*
¿desde hace cuánto tiempo? *for how long?*
el desierto *desert*
el despacho *office*
después *afterwards*
después de *after …ing*
el destino *destination*
el día *day*
el dialecto *dialect*
la diarrea *diarrhoea*
el dibujo *art, drawing*
el dibujo animado *cartoon, animated film*
diciembre *December*
los dientes *teeth*
la dieta *diet*

difícil *difficult*
digno/a *fair*
dime *tell me*
el dinero *money*
la dirección *address*
directo/a *direct*
el director *manager*
el diseñador *designer (m)*
la diseñadora *designer (f)*
el diseño *design*
disponible *available*
distinguido/a *distinguished*
divertido/a *entertaining, fun*
el documental *documentary*
el domingo *Sunday*
donde *where*
¿dónde? *where?*
dormí *I slept*
dormir *to sleep*
el dormitorio *bedroom*
las drogas *drugs*
ducharse *to have a shower*
me ducho *I shower*
me duele(n) *my … hurt(s)*
duermo *I sleep*
dulce *sweet*
durante *during*

E

e *and (before 'i' or 'hi')*
el edificio *building*
la educación física *PE*
el ejercicio *exercise*
emocionante *exciting, moving*
empezar *to begin*
empecé *I started*
empiezas *you start*
empiezo *I start*
el empleado *employee*
en *in, at, by*
me encanta(n) *I love*
encantado/a *delighted (to meet you)*
encontrar *to find*
no me encuentro bien *I don't feel well*
la energía *energy*
enero *January*
enfadarse *to get angry*
se enfadó *he/she got angry*
la enfermedad *illness*
la enfermera *nurse (f)*
el enfermero *nurse (m)*
enfermo/a *ill*
enfrente (de) *opposite*
enorme *huge*
enseñar *to teach*
equilibrado/a *balanced*
el equipo *team*
era *he/she/it was*
es *he/she/it is*
escocés/esa *Scottish*
escribir *to write*
escribir un correo *to write an email*
escribo *I write*

el escritor *writer (m)*
la escritora *writer (f)*
escuchamos *we listen, we listened*
escuchar *to listen*
escucharon *they listened*
escuché *I listened*
la escuela *school*
el espacio verde *green space*
la espalda *back*
España *Spain*
el español *Spanish (language)*
español(a) *Spanish*
esperar *to wait*
está *he/she/it is*
la estación *station*
los Estados Unidos *USA*
está *he/she/it is*
están *they are*
estar *to be*
estar de acuerdo *to agree*
estás *you are*
este/a *this*
el este *east*
el estilo *style*
estimado señor *dear sir*
el estómago *stomach*
estos/as *these*
estoy *I am*
el estudiante *student (m)*
la estudiante *student (f)*
estudiar *to study*
estupendo/a *fantastic*
el euskera *Basque (language)*
la excursión *outing*
la experiencia *experience*
experimental *experimental*
la exposición *exhibition*

F

fácil *easy*
el famoso *celebrity*
famoso/a *famous*
fatal *terrible*
favorito/a *favourite*
febrero *February*
la fecha (de nacimiento) *date (of birth)*
la fiebre *temperature, fever*
la fiesta *festival*
el fin de semana *weekend*
firmar *to sign*
el flan *creme caramel*
la flauta *flute*
la flor *flower*
el francés *French (language)*
frecuentemente *frequently*
frente a *opposite, in front of*
el frigorífico *fridge*
la frontera *border*
la fruta *fruit*
fue *he/she/it was, went*
fuera *outside*
fuerte *strong*
fui *I was, went*
fuimos *we were, went*

Vocabulario español—inglés

fumar   *to smoke*
fumé   *I smoked*
la fusión   *fusion, mixture*
el fútbol   *football*
el futbolín   *table football*
el futbolista   *footballer*
el futuro   *future*

G

la galleta   *biscuit*
ganar   *to win, earn*
tener ganas de   *to want to*
la garganta   *throat*
gastar   *to spend (money)*
genial   *great*
la gente   *people*
la geografía   *geography*
el gimnasio   *gym*
grabar   *to record*
grabó   *he/she/it recorded*
la gripe   *flu*
el grupo   *group*
guapo/a   *good-looking, attractive*
el guaraní   *Guarani (language)*
guay   *cool, great*
la guerra   *war*
la guirnalda   *garland*
la guitarra   *guitar*
me gusta(n)   *I like*
me gustaría   *I'd like to*
me gustó   *I liked*
mucho gusto   *pleased to meet you*

H

hablador(a)   *talkative*
hablar   *to speak*
hace   *he/she/it does, makes*
hace (dos años)   *(two years) ago*
hace calor   *it's hot*
hacer   *to do, make*
hago   *I do, make*
hago de canguro   *I babysit*
la hamburguesa   *hamburger*
hasta pronto   *see you soon*
hay   *there is/are*
hay que   *you have to*
he ganado   *I've won*
la hermana   *sister*
el hermano   *brother*
hice   *I did*
la hija   *daughter*
el hijo   *son, child*
la historia   *history*
hizo   *he/she/it did*
¡hola!   *hello!*
el hombre   *man*
la hora   *hour*
la hora de comer   *lunch hour*
el horario   *timetable, hours*
los horarios laborales   *working hours*
¡qué horror!   *how awful!*

hoy   *today*
el huevo   *egg*

I

de ida   *single (ticket)*
de ida y vuelta   *return (ticket)*
el idioma   *language*
importante   *important*
independiente   *independent*
infantil   *children's*
la informática   *ICT*
informativo/a   *informative*
la ingeniera   *engineer (f)*
el ingeniero   *engineer (m)*
el inglés   *English (language)*
el instituto   *school*
inteligente   *intelligent*
me interesa(n)   *I'm interested in*
interesante   *interesting*
el invierno   *winter*
ir   *to go*
ir de compras   *to go shopping*
irse   *to go away*
la isla   *island*
la izquierda   *left*

J

el jabón   *soap*
el jarabe   *syrup*
el jefe   *boss*
joven   *young*
las joyas   *jewellery*
juego   *I play (sport, game)*
el juego   *game*
el jueves   *Thursday*
el jugador   *player*
jugar a   *to play (sport, game)*
jugué   *I played*
julio   *July*
junio   *June*
justo/a   *fair*

L

el laboratorio   *(science) lab*
largo/a   *long*
¡qué lástima!   *what a pity!*
la lata   *(food/drink) can*
lavar   *to wash*
lavarse   *to wash (yourself), get washed*
lavarse los dientes   *to brush your teeth*
me lavo   *I wash*
la leche   *milk*
leer   *to read*
leo   *I read*
levantarse   *to get up*
me levanto   *I get up*
el libro   *book*
limpiar   *to clean*
llamarse   *to be called*

¿cómo te llamas?   *what's your (first) name?*
me llamo   *my name is*
la llanura   *plain*
la llegada   *arrival*
llegar   *to arrive*
llegar a tiempo   *to arrive on time*
llegué   *I arrived*
lleno/a   *full*
llevar   *to wear*
la lluvia   *rain*
luego   *then*
el lugar   *place*
el lunes   *Monday*
la luz   *light*

M

la madrastra   *stepmother*
la madrugada   *dawn*
mala suerte   *bad luck*
malo/a   *bad*
malsano/a   *unhealthy*
mañana   *tomorrow*
mandar (correos)   *to send (emails)*
la mano   *hand*
el maquillaje   *make-up*
el martes   *Tuesday*
marzo   *March*
más   *more*
más que   *more than*
más tarde   *later*
las matemáticas   *maths*
mayo   *May*
la mayoría   *majority*
la médica   *doctor (f)*
el médico   *doctor (m)*
medio/a   *average*
el medio ambiente   *environment*
en medio de   *in the middle of*
mediterráneo/a   *Mediterranean*
mejor   *better*
el/la mejor   *the best*
menos   *less*
menos que   *less than*
el mensaje   *message*
el mercado   *market*
la mesa   *table*
me toca a mí   *my turn*
mezclar   *to mix, combine*
mi(s)   *my*
el miércoles   *Wednesday*
la moda   *fashion*
la montaña   *mountain*
la moto   *motorbike*
el móvil   *mobile (phone)*
mucho   *a lot*
mucho/a   *a lot of*
las muelas   *teeth*
¡muévete!   *get moving!*
la mujer   *woman*
el mundo   *world*
el museo   *museum*
la música   *music*

muy   *very*
¡muy bien!   *well done!*

N

nacer   *to be born*
nací   *I was born*
la nacionalidad   *nationality*
nada   *nothing*
la nariz   *nose*
la natación   *swimming*
navegar (por internet)   *to surf (the internet)*
la Navidad   *Christmas*
necesitar   *to need*
ninguna parte   *nowhere*
el niño   *child (m), boy*
el nivel   *level*
no   *no, not*
no mucho   *not a lot*
la noche   *night*
la Nochebuena   *Christmas Eve*
el nombre   *first name*
la norma   *rule*
normalmente   *normally*
el norte   *north*
noviembre   *November*
nuestro/a   *our*
nunca   *never*

O

o   *or*
la obesidad   *obesity*
octubre   *October*
odio   *I hate*
el oeste   *west*
la oferta   *offer (job)*
la oficina   *office*
el oído   *ear*
el ojo   *eye*
el ordenador   *computer*
organizado/a   *organised*
el oro   *gold*
la orquesta   *orchestra*
el otoño   *autumn*
otro/a   *other*

P

paciente   *patient*
el padrastro   *stepfather*
los padres   *parents*
pagar   *to pay*
el país   *country*
el paisaje   *landscape*
el País Vasco   *the Basque Country*
el pan   *bread*
el papel   *paper*
el paquete   *packet*
para   *in order to, for*
parar   *to stop*
el parque   *park*
pasado/a   *last*

pasar   *to spend (time)*
la Pascua   *Easter*
lo pasé …   *I had a … time*
pasear   *to walk*
el pasillo   *corridor*
la pasta de dientes   *toothpaste*
el pastel   *cake*
la pastilla   *tablet*
las patatas fritas   *chips, crisps*
el patio   *playground*
el pavo   *turkey*
pedir   *to ask for*
la película   *film*
la película del Oeste   *Western*
peor   *worse*
pequeño/a   *small*
perezoso/a   *lazy*
el periódico   *newspaper*
el periodista   *journalist (m)*
la periodista   *journalist (f)*
perjudicial   *bad, harmful*
pero   *but*
el perro   *dog*
el pescado   *fish*
el petróleo   *oil, petroleum*
el pie   *foot*
la pierna   *leg*
el piloto de F1   *Formula 1 driver*
el pincho   *small portion, snack*
la piscina   *swimming pool*
planchar   *to iron*
la plantación   *plantation*
la playa   *beach*
la plaza   *square*
pobre   *poor*
la pobreza   *poverty*
un poco   *a little*
poder   *to be able to, can*
el policía   *police officer (m)*
la policía   *police officer (f)*
el polideportivo   *sports centre*
el pollo   *chicken*
poner   *to put, lay (table)*
poner en marcha   *to get underway, start*
pongo   *I put, lay*
el pop   *pop (music)*
por   *for (on behalf of), by*
por eso   *so, therefore, that's why*
por favor   *please*
por la mañana   *in the morning*
por la tarde   *in the afternoon*
por lo general   *in general*
por lo menos   *at least*
¿por qué?   *why?*
por supuesto   *of course*
por último   *finally*
el porcentaje   *percentage*
porque   *because*
práctico/a   *practical*
el precio   *price*
precioso/a   *wonderful, beautiful*
preferir   *to prefer*
prefiero   *I prefer*
la pregunta   *question*
el premio   *prize*
presentar   *to introduce*

me presento   *let me introduce myself*
prestar atención   *to pay attention*
la primavera   *spring*
primero/a   *first*
principal   *main*
principalmente   *mainly*
privado/a   *private*
probar   *to try*
el problema   *problem*
el producto verde   *green product*
el profesor   *teacher (m)*
la profesora   *teacher (f)*
el programa de deporte   *sports show*
el programa de música   *music show*
el programa de tele-realidad   *reality show*
propio/a   *own (adj)*
proteger   *to protect*
próximo/a   *next*
¡prueba!   *try!*
¡prueba otra vez!   *try again!*
pude   *I could*
el pudín de Navidad   *Christmas pudding*
pudo   *he/she/it could*
el pueblo   *village*
puede   *he/she/it can*
se puede   *you can*
puedes   *you can*
puedo   *I can*
el puente   *bridge*
pues…   *well…*
el puesto   *job, position*

Q

que   *which, that, who*
¿qué?   *what?*
¿qué haces?   *what do you do?*
¿qué hay?   *what is there?*
¿qué hiciste?   *what did you do?*
¿qué le pasa?   *what's the matter? (formal)*
¿qué ponen?   *what's on?*
¡qué suerte!   *how lucky!*
¿qué tal?   *how are you?*
¿qué te duele?   *what hurts?*
¿qué te gustaría hacer?   *what would you like to do?*
¿qué te pasa?   *what's the matter?*
el quechua   *Quechua (language)*
querer   *to want*
querido/a …   *dear …*
el queso   *cheese*
quieres   *you want*
quiero   *I want*
quizás   *perhaps*

R

rápido/a quick
un rato a while
la realidad virtual virtual reality
el recepcionista receptionist (m)
la recepcionista receptionist (f)
recibir to receive
reciclar to recycle
el recreo break (school)
reducir to reduce
regalar to give (as a present)
el regalo present
la regla rule
el remedio cure, remedy
repartir to deliver
la reserva reservation
el representante representative
se requiere it is required
el requisito requirement
residente resident
respetar to respect
restringido/a restricted
retirarse to retire
la revista magazine
revolucionario/a revolutionary
los Reyes Magos the Three Wise Men
rico/a delicious
¡qué rico/a! how delicious!
el río river
la rodilla knee
¡es un rollo! what a bore!
la ropa clothes
el ruido noise

S

el sábado Saturday
saber to know (a fact or how to do sthg)
sacar fotos to take photos
el salario salary
sale he/she/it leaves, goes out
salgo I leave, go out
salí I went out
la salida exit, departure
salió he/she/it left, went out
salir to leave, go out
el salón lounge
la salud health
le saluda atentamente yours sincerely
sano/a healthy
saqué fotos I took photos
sé I know
el secador hairdryer
sedentario/a sedentary
segundo/a second
la selva forest, jungle
la semana week
el senderismo hiking
septiembre September
ser to be
la serie de policías detective series

serio/a serious
la serpiente snake
el servicio de limpieza cleaning staff
servir to serve
siempre always
me siento I feel
siguiente following
simpático/a pleasant, nice
sin without
sin embargo however
situado/a situated
sobre about
sólo only
solo/a alone
solucionar to solve
son they are
la sopa soup
soy I'm
su(s) his, her, its
suave soft, gentle, mild
sucio/a dirty
el suelo ground
la suerte luck
la suma total
el sur south

T

también also, as well
tanto so much
la tarde afternoon, evening
el teatro drama, theatre
la tecnología technology
el telediario news (on TV)
el teléfono telephone
la telenovela soap opera
el televisor television set
temprano early
tener to have
tener hambre to be hungry
tener hijos to have children
tener que to have to
tener sed to be thirsty
tengo I have
tengo … años I'm … years old
tengo sueño I'm sleepy
tercero/a third
terminar to finish
la ternera beef, veal
el terror horror
te toca a ti your turn
el tiempo weather, time
el tiempo libre free time
la tienda shop
tienes que … you have to …
la tierra earth, ground
tímido/a shy
tinto red (wine)
típico/a typical
tirar to throw
la toalla towel
tocar to play (an instrument)
todavía still
todo/a all, every
todos los días every day
tomar to take

tonto/a stupid
¡qué tonto/a! how stupid!
la tortuga tortoise, turtle
la tos cough
trabajador(a) hard-working
trabajar to work
trabajo I work
trabajó he/she worked
el trabajo job
traducir to translate
traduzco I translate
traer to bring
el tráfico traffic
trágico/a tragic
el transporte público public transport
trata de it's about
¿de qué trata? what is it about?
tratar de to be about
el tren train
se ha triplicado it has tripled
la trompeta trumpet
tuve I had
tuviste you had
tuvo he/she/it had

U

último/a last
el uniforme uniform
usar to use
útil useful
útilizar to use

V

las vacaciones holidays
vale OK
valiente brave
el valle valley
valorar to value, rate
la variedad variety
ve he/she/it sees
a veces sometimes
vemos we see, watch
vender to sell
veo I see, watch
ver to see, watch
a ver… well…, let's see
el verano summer
las verduras vegetables
una vez al día once a day
en vez de instead of
de vez en cuando from time to time
vi I saw, watched
viajar to travel
el viaje journey
la vida life
el vidrio glass
el viernes Friday
vino he/she/it came
el vino wine
vio he/she/it saw, watched
el violín violin

vivir   *to live*
vivo   *I live*
el volcán   *volcano*
el voleibol   *volleyball*
volver   *to return*
volvió   *he/she returned*
tengo vómitos   *I've been sick*
voy   *I go*
voy a …   *I'm going to …*
la voz   *voice*

Y

y   *and*
el yogur   *yoghurt*

Z

las zapatillas de deporte   *trainers*
los zapatos   *shoes*

A

to be able to   *poder*
about   *sobre*
afternoon   *la tarde*
afterwards   *después*
to agree   *estar de acuerdo*
all   *todo/a*
almost   *casi*
alone   *solo/a*
also   *también*
I am   *estoy, soy*
April   *abril*
they are   *están, son*
we are   *estamos, somos*
you are   *estás, eres*
arm   *el brazo*
arrival   *la llegada*
to arrive   *llegar*
I arrived   *llegué*
art   *el dibujo*
to ask for   *pedir*
aspirin   *la aspirina*
at least   *por lo menos*
attractive   *guapo/a*
August   *agosto*
autumn   *el otoño*

B

back   *la espalda*
bad   *malo/a*
to be   *estar, ser*
because   *porque*
bed   *la cama*
bedroom   *el dormitorio*
to begin   *empezar*
the best   *el/la mejor*
better   *mejor*
body   *el cuerpo*
book   *el libro*
boring   *aburrido/a*
bread   *el pan*
break   *el recreo (school)*
brother   *el hermano*
to brush your teeth   *lavarse los dientes*
building   *el edificio*
business studies   *el comercio*
but   *pero*
to buy   *comprar*

C

to be called   *llamarse*
he/she/it
   can   *puede*
I can   *puedo*
you can   *puedes*
   cartoon   *los dibujos animados*
to charge   *cargar*
to chat online   *chatear*
   chess   *el ajedrez*
   chewing gum   *el chicle*
   chips   *las patatas fritas*

choir   *el coro*
cigarette   *el cigarrillo*
cinema   *el cine*
city   *la ciudad*
to clean   *limpiar*
clothes   *la ropa*
coffee   *el café*
cold   *el catarro*
comedy   *la comedia*
comfortable   *cómodo/a*
computer   *el ordenador*
concert   *el concierto*
cook   *el cocinero/la cocinera*
cool   *guay*
cough   *la tos*
he/she/it
   could   *pudo*
I could   *pude*
   country   *el país*

D

dance   *el baile*
to dance   *bailar*
date (of birth)   *la fecha (de nacimiento)*
day   *el día*
the day before yesterday   *anteayer*
dear …   *querido/a …*
dear sir   *estimado señor*
December   *diciembre*
delicious   *rico/a*
design   *el diseño*
detective series   *la serie de policías*
diarrhoea   *la diarrea*
he/she/it
   did   *hizo*
I did   *hice*
   diet   *la dieta*
   difficult   *difícil*
   dining hall/room   *el comedor*
I do   *hago*
to do   *hacer*
   doctor   *el médico/la médica*
   documentary   *el documental*
he/she/it
   does   *hace*
to download   *descargar*
   drama   *el teatro*
   drink   *la bebida*
to drink   *beber*
   drugs   *las drogas*
   during   *durante*

E

each   *cada*
ear   *el oído*
early   *temprano*
east   *el este*
easy   *fácil*
to eat   *comer*
engineer   *el ingeniero/ la ingeniera*
English   *el inglés (language)*

enough   *bastante*
entertaining   *divertido/a*
environment   *el medio ambiente*
evening   *la tarde*
every   *todo/a, todos/as*
every day   *todos los días*
exciting   *emocionante*
exercise   *el ejercicio*
exit   *la salida*
eye   *el ojo*

F

face   *la cara*
fair   *justo/a*
fair trade   *el comercio justo*
famous   *famoso/a*
fantastic   *¡bomba!, estupendo/a*
fashion   *la moda*
fast food   *la comida rápida*
favourite   *favorito/a*
February   *febrero*
film   *la película*
finally   *por último*
to find   *encontrar*
fine   *bien*
finger   *el dedo*
to finish   *terminar*
first   *primero/a*
first name   *el nombre*
flu   *la gripe*
food   *el alimento, la comida*
foot   *el pie*
for (on behalf of)   *por*
for (time)   *desde hace*
for how long?   *¿desde hace cuánto tiempo?*
free time   *el tiempo libre*
French   *el francés (language)*
Friday   *el viernes*
friend   *el amigo/la amiga*
from   *a partir de*
from time to time   *de vez en cuando*
fruit   *la fruta*
fun   *divertido/a*
future   *el futuro*

G

game   *el juego*
game show   *el concurso*
garden   *el jardín*
geography   *la geografía*
German   *el alemán (language)*
to get up   *levantarse*
I go   *voy*
to go   *ir*
to go shopping   *ir de compras*
to go to bed   *acostarse*
good   *bueno/a*
greasy   *grasiento/a*
great   *genial, guay, ¡qué bien!*
gym   *el gimnasio*

H

I had *tuve*
you had *tuviste*
hairdryer *el secador*
hand *la mano*
hard-working *trabajador(a)*
I have *tengo*
to have *tener*
to have a shower *ducharse*
to have breakfast *desayunar*
to have dinner *cenar*
to have to *tener que, deber*
head *la cabeza*
health *la salud*
healthy *sano/a*
to help *ayudar*
high *alto/a*
holidays *las vacaciones*
homework *los deberes*
house *la casa*
how? *¿cómo?*
how are you? *¿qué tal?*
how many? *¿cuántos/as?*
how much? *¿cuánto/a?*
to be hungry *tener hambre*
to hurt *doler*

I

ICT *la informática*
ill *enfermo/a*
illness *la enfermedad*
in *en*
instead of *en vez de*
to be introduced *presentarse*
he/she/it
is *está, es*

J

January *enero*
job *el trabajo*
journalist *el periodista/ la periodista*
journey *el viaje*
July *julio*
June *junio*
junk food *la comida basura*

K

kitchen *la cocina*
knee *la rodilla*
I know *sé*
to know (a fact or how to do sthg) *saber*
to know (a person or place) *conocer*

L

language *el idioma*
last *pasado/a*
lazy *perezoso/a*
to leave *dejar, salir*
left *la izquierda*
leg *la pierna*
less *menos*
lesson *la clase*
let's see *a ver*
library *la biblioteca*
I like *me gusta(n)*
I'd like to *me gustaría*
to listen (to) *escuchar*
to look for *buscar*
a lot *mucho*
a lot of *mucho/a, muchos/as*
lunch hour *la hora de comer*

M

magazine *la revista*
to make *hacer*
make-up *el maquillaje*
March *marzo*
maths *las matemáticas*
May *mayo*
meat *la carne*
milk *la leche*
mobile *el móvil*
Monday *el lunes*
money *el dinero*
more *más*
mouth *la boca*
moving *emocionante*
museum *el museo*
music *la música*
music show *el programa de música*
I must *debo*
you must *debes*
my *mi(s)*

N

my name is *me llamo*
nasty *antipático/a*
nationality *la nacionalidad*
never *nunca*
news (on TV) *el telediario*
newspaper *el periódico*
next *próximo/a*
next year *el año que viene*
nice *bonito/a, simpático/a*
night *la noche*
north *el norte*
nose *la nariz*
not *no*
nothing *nada*
November *noviembre*
now *ahora*
nowhere *ninguna parte*
nurse *el enfermero/ la enfermera*

O

October *octubre*
of course *por supuesto*
office *el despacho, la oficina*
often *a menudo*
OK *vale*
old *antiguo/a*
once a day *una vez al día*
opposite *enfrente, frente a*
or *o*
organised *organizado/a*
other *otro/a*
our *nuestro/a*

P

parents *los padres*
patient *paciente*
to pay *pagar*
PE *la educación física*
people *la gente*
perhaps *quizás*
place *el lugar*
platform *el andén*
to play (a sport/game) *jugar a*
to play (an instrument) *tocar*
playground *el patio*
pleasant *simpático/a*
please *por favor*
pleased to meet you *mucho gusto*
poor *pobre*
practical *práctico/a*
to prefer *preferir*
present *el regalo*
price *el precio*
private *privado/a*
problem *el problema*
pupil *el alumno*
to put *poner*

R

rain *la lluvia*
to read *leer*
real *auténtico/a*
reality show *el programa de tele-realidad*
to recycle *reciclar*
to reduce *reducir*
return (ticket) *(el billete) de ida y vuelta*
right *la derecha*
room *la habitación, la sala*
rubbish *la basura*
rule *la norma*
to run *correr*

S

salary *el salario*
Saturday *el sábado*
to save (money) *ahorrar*

Vocabulario inglés—español

to say *decir*
school *la escuela, el instituto*
science(s) *las ciencias*
sci-fi *la ciencia-ficción*
to see *ver*
see you soon *hasta pronto*
to sell *vender*
to send (emails) *mandar (correos)*
September *septiembre*
serious *serio/a*
I should *debería*
you should *deberías*
shy *tímido/a*
to be sick *tener vómitos*
to sing *cantar*
singer *el cantante/ la cantante*
single (ticket) *(el billete) de ida*
sister *la hermana*
to sleep *dormir*
small *pequeño/a*
soap *el jabón*
soap opera *la telenovela*
some *alguno/a*
someone *alguien*
sometimes *a veces*
south *el sur*
Spanish *el español (language)*
to speak *hablar*
to spend (money) *gastar*
to spend (time) *pasar*
sport *el deporte*
sports show *el programa de deporte*
spring *la primavera*
station *la estación*
still *todavía*
stomach *el estómago*
street *la calle*
strict *severo/a*
student *el estudiante/ la estudiante*
to study *estudiar*
stupid *tonto/a*
subject *la asignatura*
summer *el verano*
Sunday *el domingo*
to surf the internet *navegar por internet*
surname *el apellido*
swimming *la natación*
swimming pool *la piscina*
syrup *el jarabe*

T

tablet *la pastilla*
to take *tomar*
to take photos *sacar fotos*
talkative *hablador(a)*
teacher *el profesor/ la profesora*
team *el equipo*
technology *la tecnología*
teeth *las muelas, los dientes*

telephone *el teléfono*
temperature *la fiebre*
that *que*
theatre *el teatro*
then *luego*
there is/are *hay*
these *estos/as*
to be thirsty *tener sed*
this *este/a*
throat *la garganta*
Thursday *el jueves*
ticket *el billete*
timetable *el horario*
tired *cansado/a*
to *a, para*
today *hoy*
tomorrow *mañana*
too much *demasiado/a*
toothbrush *el cepillo de dientes*
toothpaste *la pasta de dientes*
towel *la toalla*
train *el tren*
trainers *las zapatillas de deporte*
T-shirt *la camiseta*
Tuesday *el martes*

U

unhealthy *malsano/a*
uniform *el uniforme*
unpleasant *antipático/a*
to use *usar*
useful *útil*

V

vegetables *las verduras*
very *muy*
village *el pueblo*
voice *la voz*

W

waiter/waitress *el camarero/ la camarera*
I want *quiero*
to want *querer*
you want *quieres*
he/she/it
was *fue*
I was *fui*
to wash *lavar(se)*
to watch *ver*
water *el agua (f)*
to wear *llevar*
weather *el tiempo*
Wednesday *el miércoles*
week *la semana*
weekend *el fin de semana*
well *pues*

he/she/it
went *fue*
I went *fui*
west *el oeste*
what? *¿qué?*
what do you do? *¿qué haces?*
what is there? *¿qué hay?*
what time? *¿a qué hora?*
what's on? *¿qué ponen?*
what's the matter? *¿qué te pasa?*
when *cuando*
when? *¿cuándo?*
where? *¿dónde?*
which? *¿cuál(es)?*
why? *¿por qué?*
to win *ganar*
winter *el invierno*
with *con*
wonderful *precioso/a*
to work *trabajar*
worse *peor*
the worst *el/la peor*
to write *escribir*

Y

yesterday *ayer*
young *joven*
yours sincerely *le saluda atentamente*